Knowing Who I Am

Knowing Who I Am

A Black Entrepreneur's Struggle and Success in the American South

Earl M. Middleton

with Joy W. Barnes

The University of South Carolina Press

Published by the University of South Carolina Press
Columbia, South Carolina 29208

www.sc.edu/uscpress

Manufactured in the United States of America

17 16 15 14 13 12 11 10 09 08   10 9 8 7 6 5 4 3 2 1

Library of Congress Cataloging-in-Publication Data

Middleton, Earl M., 1919–
    Knowing who I am : a Black entrepreneur's struggle and success in the American
South / Earl M. Middleton, with Joy W. Barnes.
        p. cm.
    Includes bibliographical references and index.
    ISBN-13: 978-1-57003-715-3 (cloth : alk. paper)
    ISBN-10: 1-57003-715-9 (cloth : alk. paper)
        1. Middleton, Earl M., 1919– 2. African American businesspeople—South
Carolina.—Biography. 3. Businessmen—South Carolina—Biography. 4. African
American legislators—South Carolina—Biography. 5. Legislators—South Carolina
Biography. 6. South Carolina. General Assembly. House of Representatives—
Biography. 7. African Americans—South Carolina—Social conditions—20th
century. 8. World War, 1939–1945—Participation, African American. 9. South
Carolina—Social conditions—20th century. 10. South Carolina—Biography.
I. Barnes, Joy W., 1939– II. Title.
E185.93.S7M47 2008
338.092—dc22   2007043037

To the memory of my grandfather Abram Middleton,
my parents, Samuel Edgar and Ella Govan Middleton,
and my beloved wife, Bernice Bryant Middleton

Contents

Illustrations

Preface

Writing a memoir never occurred to me until a few years ago. Everyone's life memories, whether positive or negative, are meaningful to them, but at what point are they significant enough to put into writing? The answer could depend on an individual's orientation. For a person steeped in genealogical research, for example, writing a memoir is almost de rigueur. Although that certainly does not describe me, there were indicators that kept coming to the surface, encouraging me to write down my memories.

In the 1970s, when I was serving in the South Carolina legislature, one of my fellow House members, the late Sam Manning from Spartanburg, was a historian. I showed Sam some of my grandfather's journals, and Sam influenced me to place copies of Abram Middleton's day-by-day comments at the University of South Carolina's South Caroliniana Library. More than thirty years later, when the originals had been misplaced, I had access to the copies at that library. Abram was a Methodist minister, and I learned that the church had required their ministers to keep journals. That was one indicator for me.

In the 1980s my cousin Mamie Garvin Fields published her *Lemon Swamp and Other Places: A Carolina Memoir.* Her book, written with the assistance of her granddaughter Karen Fields, was well received and merited a review in the *Wall Street Journal.* Mamie's work was a benchmark for me.

In 1992 the *Wall Street Journal* did a front-page article on the success of my family's real estate business. The positive ripple effects are still coming from people interested in our story. That too was a signal.

I began to think that someday my descendants might be as interested in me as I am in those who came before me. By that time Joy Barnes and I were putting feelers out about doing my memoir, and almost everyone we spoke with encouraged me to go forward.

The fact that I'm black entered into the decision as well. We searched the literature for published memoirs by black men of achievement in fields other than sports and entertainment. We found fewer than two dozen. The tipping point in my decision came when someone said, "Sometimes it is much easier for a young black boy to identify success with a black man who is relatively unknown than it is to identify with a famous person. It seems more possible for him. It's the 'If he can do it, I can do it' attitude they can relate to." Knowing who I am compels me to share my positive life experiences with others.

This was the evolution of my book. I hope that readers will enjoy it as much as Joy Barnes and I enjoyed the endeavor.

Acknowledgments

We recognize Richard Pine, a prominent New York literary agent, for telling us first that Earl Middleton's situation was worthy of a book. We also thank Tony Burroughs, genealogy consultant extraordinaire, for emphasizing the urgency of completing this memoir. Conversations with several friends helped us in relating our accounts of incidents, people, and places. Among those friends are Dr. Clemmie E. Webber, Robert Howard, the late Alexander Lewis, Dr. Alba M. (Mrs. Alexander) Lewis, Lamar Dawkins Sr., and the late Leroy Sulton. For providing names and sketches of founding VFW Post 8166 members, we acknowledge the present membership. For providing the names of many of the soldiers and officers at Maxwell Air Force Base, Alabama, during World War II, we are most grateful to the late Morton B. Howell.

Dr. Allen Stokes, Dr. Tom Johnson, Robin Copp, and Henry Fulmer at the South Caroliniana Library, University of South Carolina, were generous in helping us locate research materials, as was Steve Tuttle at the South Carolina Department of Archives and History. Miss Edith Frederick at the H. V. Manning Library, Claflin University, has been an ongoing source of help in the research for this book. Thanks also to Barbara Doyle for sharing some of the knowledge she has gleaned during her many years as historian at Middleton Place.

For reading early drafts and providing feedback, we express our gratitude to Dr. Theodore Rosengarten, Dr. Walter Edgar, Dr. Mary Eugenia W. Sanders, Arthur D. Middleton, and Dr. Sam Watson. For her gracious help with the layout, typing, and binding of the proposal for this book, we thank Dr. Hajar Sanders. We appreciate Mrs. Angie Davis's hours of transcription work from tapes that Earl Middleton has recorded through the years. We thank all our friends who've helped and encouraged us.

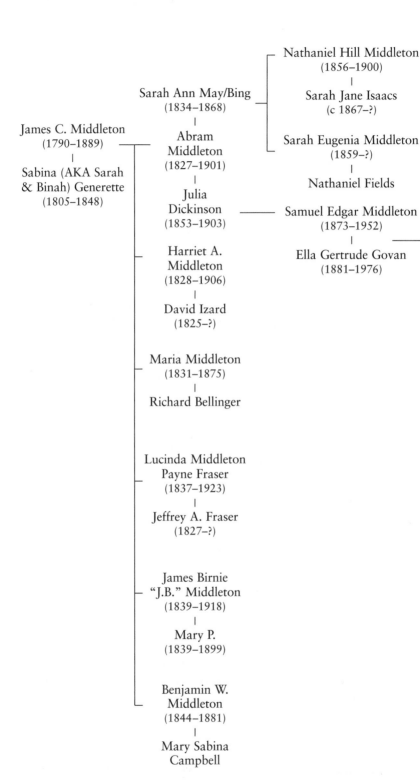

James C. Middleton
(1790–1889)
|
Sabina (AKA Sarah
& Binah) Generette
(1805–1848)

Sarah Ann May/Bing
(1834–1868)
|
Abram
Middleton
(1827–1901)
|
Julia
Dickinson
(1853–1903)

Harriet A.
Middleton
(1828–1906)
|
David Izard
(1825–?)

Maria Middleton
(1831–1875)
|
Richard Bellinger

Lucinda Middleton
Payne Fraser
(1837–1923)
|
Jeffrey A. Fraser
(1827–?)

James Birnie
"J.B." Middleton
(1839–1918)
|
Mary P.
(1839–1899)

Benjamin W.
Middleton
(1844–1881)
|
Mary Sabina
Campbell

Nathaniel Hill Middleton
(1856–1900)
|
Sarah Jane Isaacs
(c 1867–?)

Sarah Eugenia Middleton
(1859–?)
|
Nathaniel Fields

Samuel Edgar Middleton
(1873–1952)
|
Ella Gertrude Govan
(1881–1976)

Descendants of James C. Middleton

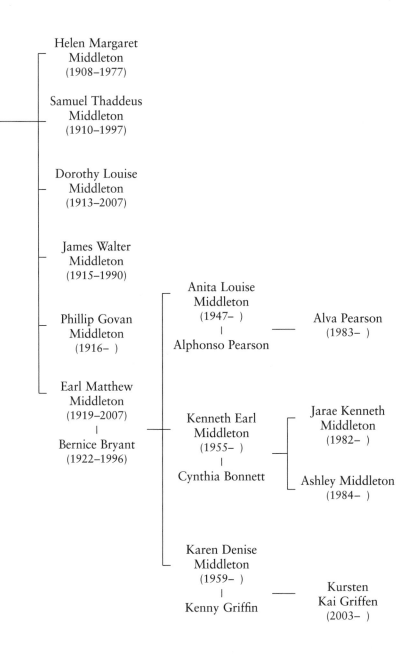

Helen Margaret
Middleton
(1908–1977)

Samuel Thaddeus
Middleton
(1910–1997)

Dorothy Louise
Middleton
(1913–2007)

James Walter
Middleton
(1915–1990)

Phillip Govan
Middleton
(1916–)

Earl Matthew
Middleton
(1919–2007)
|
Bernice Bryant
(1922–1996)

Anita Louise
Middleton
(1947–)
|
Alphonso Pearson

Alva Pearson
(1983–)

Kenneth Earl
Middleton
(1955–)
|
Cynthia Bonnett

Jarae Kenneth
Middleton
(1982–)

Ashley Middleton
(1984–)

Karen Denise
Middleton
(1959–)
|
Kenny Griffin

Kursten
Kai Griffen
(2003–)

Part One

―――∞∞∞―――

Slavery to the Great Depression

1

Ancestors

Joseph Bellinger died on January 10, 1830, in Charleston, South Carolina. The prominent lowcountry planter had served in the South Carolina legislature for twelve years and the U.S. Congress for one term. More important to me, Mr. Bellinger had owned a three-year-old boy named Abram. When Mr. Bellinger's estate was appraised, Abram's worth was put at $90. His value appeared on the same line with three mules that were valued at $150. Evidently, in the appraisers' opinion, Abram was worth $40 more than a mule. However, they didn't think he was worth as much as Mr. Bellinger's carriage and harness, which they valued at $150. Abram was my grandfather.

Thirty-eight years later, into his third year of freedom after a great national war had ended slavery, Abram Middleton was serving as a delegate to the 1868 South Carolina Constitutional Convention. He wrote a letter to the appraiser of the old estate, Charles R. Carroll, and reported on the proceedings as well as some business matters. Although Granddaddy was very respectful, his tone made it clear that he had become Mr. Carroll's peer.

Charles Rivers Carroll was a highly esteemed attorney residing in Midway, Barnwell District. He was a neighbor, friend, and mentor to the South Carolina literary giant William Gilmore Simms, who was the most prolific southern antebellum writer and widely acclaimed in his day. Attorney Carroll was my grandfather's senior by nearly thirty years. He was related to the Bellingers by his marriage to Sarah Fishburne, whose mother was Mary Cussings Bellinger. Their son, Francis Fishburne Carroll, who was close to Granddaddy in age, became a medical doctor.

Edmund Cussings Bellinger, son of Joseph Bellinger, inherited his father's property, including Abram, in 1830 when Edmund was only sixteen. When Edmund C. Bellinger died on December 9, 1848, Charles Rivers Carroll became the primary executor of his estate.

The death of a slave owner could mark a perilous time for the slaves in his or her ownership. As the owner's property was bequeathed to the heirs, slave families could be broken up. Under the terms of Edmund C. Bellinger's December 8, 1848, will, however, the bulk of his estate was to remain intact until his son, Joseph, reached twenty-one years of age in 1860. For this reason Charles R. Carroll was the person acting on behalf of the owner's estate and had the ultimate say about all the assets, including Abram and our other family members. Evidently Charles Carroll had trust in my grandfather because his son, Dr. Francis Carroll, sold Granddaddy property in Midway in 1868, a few months after the South Carolina Constitutional Convention.

Abram Middleton became an accomplished person and a leader of men. Though a slave, he had learned to read and write, and while held in bondage he built a business as a tailor and a master carpenter. After the Civil War he enrolled at Baker Theological School in Charleston and received his credentials, becoming a Methodist Episcopal minister. In 1868 he built a home for his family on the land he purchased from Dr. Carroll. One of Abram's sons, born during slavery, became a medical doctor after the Civil War. In 1869 Abram was selected as a founding trustee of Claflin University in Orangeburg, South Carolina. He served in that position and as a Methodist minister until he died in 1901.

According to Abram Middleton's family Bible (owned in 2006 by his descendent Pauline Mansfield of East Point, Georgia), Abram was first married in 1851 to a light-skinned free woman named Sarah Ann Bing. She bore him six children, two of whom lived to maturity. Sarah died in 1868. Two years later Abram married my grandmother, Julia Dickinson from Buford's Bridge, South Carolina, who would bear him eleven children.

Abram had brothers who were leaders too. James B. Middleton was also a Baker Theological School graduate and a Methodist minister. He served as secretary of the South Carolina Conference from 1882 through 1913. In addition "Uncle J.B." was a prolific writer, publishing many serious articles in Methodist newspapers. He was chairman of the board of trustees of the Methodist-sponsored Sterling College in Greenville, South Carolina.

Abram's younger brother, Benjamin W. Middleton, was postmaster at Midway, South Carolina, from 1870 until 1872, when he was elected to the S.C. House of Representatives. He served in the House until 1874. During this period in our state's history the S.C. House and Senate were referred to as "the Reconstruction Legislature." During the Reconstruction period that followed the Civil War and lasted less than a decade, blacks, many of whom had been enslaved, were given most of the rights of free people, including the right to vote and hold public office. After one term in the S.C. House, Benjamin Middleton served a year as Barnwell County school commissioner until 1876.

Abram spent about half his life in slavery and half as a free man. His postwar ministry took him to various parts of eastern South Carolina, including the lowcountry, Pee Dee, and Midlands areas. After he became a minister, Abram used his knowledge and skills as a builder to construct twenty-eight churches, while he remodeled and improved many other churches and parsonages. On his deathbed he told my father that he was leaving him his property on Clark Street in Orangeburg and in return wanted him to make sure that each of Papa's brothers and sisters got an education. That agreement would come back to haunt my father and work a severe financial hardship on our family. Papa never went to college himself, but he saw to it that his brothers and sisters did.

The origin of the Middleton surname in my family is still being researched. We know that when Abram Middleton married Sarah Bing, a free woman, in 1851, she immediately began appearing on the records as Sarah Middleton. This proves that we had the Middleton name in slave times. E. C. Bellinger became the owner of great-grandfather James C. Middleton sometime between 1830 and 1848. Lowcountry planter families such as the Bellingers and the Middletons had many interactions, including marriages. Thus James C. may have belonged to a Middleton before he came into Bellinger's possession. Possibly a member of a third planter family was involved in the transfer as well. A likely possibility would have been Lucia Bellinger Pinckney, sister of the first Joseph Bellinger and executor of his estate, who was married to Miles Brewton Pinckney, a Charleston lawyer.

My father, Samuel Edgar Middleton, was Abram Middleton's third child by his second wife, Julia Dickinson Middleton. He was born in 1873 in Midway, in the part of Barnwell County that is now in Bamberg County, near one of the plantations that belonged to my grandfather's owners, the Bellingers. My mother, Ella Govan Middleton, was the daughter of a

Baptist preacher, Paul Govan, and his wife, Margaret Ancrum Govan. They had four daughters. Mama graduated from South Carolina State College in 1903, several years before she married Papa. She taught school in Orangeburg. The Govans had lived next door to the Middletons on Goff Avenue before the Middletons moved to Clark Street.

Orangeburg became home to Abram's branch of the Middleton family because of Claflin University. Claflin was chartered in 1869, when the South Carolina Conference of the Methodist Episcopal Church realized that, to carry forward the work of the church, laymen as well as ministers must be educated. The idea for a higher grade of education for freedman and others in the South was made real by the Honorable Lee Claflin and his son William Claflin, governor of Massachusetts, who provided the money to purchase the Orangeburg site from the former Orangeburg Female College. Granddaddy, as a trustee at Claflin who never missed a meeting, found it necessary to be in Orangeburg so much on university business that he moved his home to be within walking distance. For some years the school received some financial support from the State of South Carolina.

The history of Orangeburg includes its strategic role during the Revolutionary War, with the governor's office temporarily established at the Donald Bruce House in 1780. The railroad reached Orangeburg in 1840. Union general William T. Sherman came through in 1865 with his army and burned much of the town before he left. Reconstruction was a difficult period, and the effects have been felt for generations since.

In 1896, with the passage of the Morrill Act and segregation of the races, S.C. State was formed as an agricultural and mechanical school. The great educator Booker T. Washington saw this as the area in which blacks could make the biggest leaps in their lives. S.C. State became a state-supported college primarily for the education of blacks in South Carolina, and Claflin remained private with support and sponsorship continuing from the Methodist Church. After the separation of the two schools in 1896, Claflin emphasized the arts and intellectualism more in its course offerings. This was in keeping with the ideas of the great intellectual giant W. E. B. Du Bois as to the most advantageous route for black advancement in America. The establishment of Claflin, S.C. State, and Orangeburg-Calhoun Technical Education College in 1969 were high points in the county's educational history.

People in this area suffered during the Great Depression much as families in other areas of the country did. During World War II an air base was constructed near the Orangeburg County town of North, and a pilot-training facility just south of Orangeburg prepared four thousand Americans and sixteen hundred French aviators for service. After the war tourism increased, and U.S. 301 was the main route from New York to Florida until Interstate 95 was opened in 1977. Primary and secondary education have undergone difficult advances in my lifetime and are still being improved.

Orangeburg is the county seat, has always had an agricultural base, and is in the center of a county (also Orangeburg) whose land size measures 1,106 square miles. The county's 2007 population is close to 100,000 people. More than 55,000 people live within six miles of downtown Orangeburg, although the municipality officially has a population of only 12,765 residents because its corporate boundary has changed little in thirty years. City leaders seem to be in the mood to change that through annexation so that the statistics will more nearly fit the reality that Orangeburg is a small city with a diversified local economy that includes international manufacturing concerns, a world-renowned rose garden, golf courses, an airport, a water park, a municipal auditorium, a utilities department, and a respected public safety department. Dr. Mobley's hospital has grown to become the highly rated 286-bed, acute-care Regional Medical Center, with close-by access to Interstates 26 and 95. In addition Orangeburg is home to the largest community health facility in South Carolina, the Family Health Centers.

Because Orangeburg is the largest population center between Columbia in the Midlands and Charleston on the coast, residents have access to everything needed for day-to-day living. It is not necessary to travel to another shopping area unless you are seeking luxury goods. My family has been at home in Orangeburg for five generations, with my son and his wife choosing to raise their family here.

Papa was forty-six years old when I was born on February 18, 1919, in Orangeburg, twenty miles north of his birthplace. That was the year the city was welcoming home World War I veterans and the chamber of commerce announced that Dr. Charles Mobley would open a hospital in town. It was also the year that the National Association for the Advancement of Colored People (NAACP) held a national conference on lynching.

Mama, whose family was also from Orangeburg, was Papa's third wife (his first two died), and I was their youngest child. I was born in the two-story house on Clark Street, the property Granddaddy gave Papa on his deathbed. It still stands today across the highway from Claflin

University's Jonas T. Kennedy Center. Evidently Granddaddy was responsible for getting our house built before he died in 1901.

Papa learned carpentry skills from his father. When I was very young I remember Papa walking each day to and from his job in Rowesville, ten miles from where we lived. That meant Papa walked twenty miles every day to get to work and back. He and Mama never owned an automobile. I can still see Papa putting his carpenter bags over his shoulders and heading out the door. Later in his life Papa was an instructor in the manual training department at Claflin University for sixteen years and then was an instructor in the woodwork department at South Carolina State College for twenty-one years. At State College Papa was affectionately known as "Cap" Middleton. When Papa died in 1952, Mama continued living in the house on Clark Street, where she boarded college girls. After she was too old to live alone Mama lived with my sister Helen.

My parents made it clear that, as Middletons, we were important people, as good as anyone else. We were not supposed to do certain things that might reflect negatively on ourselves or our family. We were black people with a history, and we knew that our grandfather was a minister and that he could read and write during slavery times. From my earliest years I've had a sense of knowing who I am. It was made clear to us that along with being a Middleton came responsibilities. These included awareness of the needs of others around us, attending to God and church, being personally accountable for our schoolwork, helping our parents with household and yard chores, and maintaining good character.

In South Carolina the Middleton name is associated with the founding of our country. Henry Middleton was president of the First Continental Congress and one of the wealthiest people in the colonies. His son Arthur was one of the signers of the Declaration of Independence. Arthur's son Henry was governor of South Carolina and U.S. minister to Russia. Of course, these were white Middletons, but we knew that since they were from Charleston there was most likely a connection.

Mama made sure that all of us went to school. We had to go. There wasn't any question about our going to college; we were going and that was it. I guess the fact that Mama was one of the early graduates of S.C. State College and had taught school gave her the advantage of knowing the value of an education. At the same time that Mama was emphasizing the importance of education, it was made known to my brothers and sisters and me that we were not "above" others whose circumstances might be different than ours. Our family was not rich in material assets; in fact, my parents were constantly scraping to keep us fed, clothed, and housed and to make sure we were educated. But we were rich in the intangibles of life. Our heritage was firmly rooted in Christian values acquired by our ancestors during slavery.

As we grew up Mama managed our home and us kids. Papa let Mama handle the finances, and he stood behind whatever decisions she made. He turned his earnings over to her, and she took it from there. Mama was a genius handling the meager amount of money Papa was able to earn during the Depression years. Papa's salary when he worked at State College was sixty-five dollars a month. We were thankful to have anything coming in as we witnessed other families with no income at all during those times.

Mama bought groceries and supplies for the house from Maxwell's on Russell Street near the "Railroad Corner." She had an account there and would pay our bills on the first of the month when Papa received his paycheck. John M. Maxwell was an excellent businessman. His grocery store was one of the most successful black businesses in Orangeburg. He was a trustee, as was Papa, of the church my family belonged to, Trinity United Methodist. His daughter, Cassandra, became the first black female attorney in South Carolina.

At that time probably the largest black-owned business in Orangeburg was Sulton Lumber Mill. This was a significant enterprise because of the volume of the company's sales, the number of its employees, and the customer base it served. Some years later Carlson Austin became a very successful black businessman in Orangeburg. Through his own ingenuity he built a thriving enterprise in home appliances. One of my Claflin classmates, Ellsworth Whaley, was the daughter of an extremely successful agribusinessman, "Pink" Whaley, in nearby St. Matthews. Unfortunately, while we were students at Claflin, she lost her father in a still-unsolved murder. Mr. Murray from the town of Bowman was another progressive businessman in the area. He started as a farmer and built a large portfolio of rental properties. I remember, too, that Laval Dash was the owner of an early cab company in Orangeburg. It is important to note that, even though I was growing up black in the South, I did have some inspiration from successful black men and could pattern myself after them.

Our house was within walking distance of Maxwell's store. The roads were not paved then. We had electricity in our house on Clark Street and a well in the yard for drinking water. We had an outhouse, and there was a tin tub inside the house where we took our baths. An icebox in a back-porch pantry kept food fresh. Once a week the iceman, who was black, would deliver a large block of ice for the icebox compartment. To keep the block from melting too quickly we would cover it with sawdust. Then when we needed ice we'd brush off the sawdust and chisel off the desired amount with the ice pick.

The living room, dining room, kitchen, and two bedrooms were on the first floor, along with front and back porches. Upstairs we had three bedrooms, but only one was finished. All the fireplaces were downstairs. A large photograph of Granddaddy Middleton hung over the fireplace mantel in the living room. At times the roof leaked, and Granddaddy's picture still has the resulting water stains. The house was constructed of wood, including wooden shingles on the roof. Some of the lumber may have come from a church that had been demolished.

Mama made curtains for the windows. She had a Singer sewing machine, which she used constantly. In those days making clothes at home was a necessary task. One could not go to a store and buy clothes off a rack as we do today. Mama taught my sisters, Helen Margaret and Dorothy Louise, how to sew too. All of us were assigned household chores and yard work. You might say that Papa was the CEO of the Middleton family, and he in turn delegated to Mama his authority with regard to the house and us children. She divided up the work, giving the inside work to the girls and the outside chores to the boys. The girls prepared the food, washed curtains, cleaned rugs, and scrubbed floors in the house and on the porch. It seemed that this was the way most of the black families we knew structured their household chores when we were growing up. All the children had to work at domestic chores. From what we could tell, the well-off whites did not require this type of work from their children, so as soon as we were old enough we took odd jobs doing similar work around their homes. We would, however, see white boys working at delivering newspapers.

All the outside work was the responsibility of my brothers and me. For starters we worked in the garden. I especially remember the hoeing. Growing a lot of our vegetables and fruits was absolutely necessary to having an adequate food supply for a family of ten people. Fortunately Orangeburg has a long growing season—usually about nine months. If we didn't finish our hoeing before school, we had to complete it later in the day after school time.

Mama would can enough vegetables and fruits to get us through the winter. She used Mason jars with two-piece, screw-top lids. All winter long we were able to enjoy the results of our harvest—green beans, okra, toma-toes, peas, potatoes, carrots, onions, corn, and squash, plus peaches, figs, pears, and apples. We also harvested cold-weather vegetables such as cab-bage and collard greens and enjoyed pecans from the trees in our yard.

In addition to gardening, my brothers and I had to cut all the wood. Wood was used for all the cooking and heating in our home. We had four fireplaces in the house plus the cooking stove. In the winter the fires would burn during the day but not at night, when we would cover up with lots of blankets and quilts for warmth. Then new fires would be started again the next morning. We also used wood in any outside fires for cooking or hot water. Needless to say, sawing and chopping the wood was a huge job for my brothers and me. We worked on that every day year 'round. Wood was delivered to our house by the cord—that's 128 cubic feet as arranged in a pile 8 feet long, 4 feet high, and 4 feet wide. We had a crosscut saw and a "woodhorse," and we would cut the wood, split it up with the ax, and stack it on the back porch.

Raking the yard was also the boys' responsibility. We had large pecan trees that shed leaves in profusion. The constant raking gave the yard a neat appearance, and passersby frequently complimented us on it. To Mama and Papa it represented the order and discipline they were teach-ing us.

During most of my boyhood we had the Brower sisters—Rossie and Eleanor—living with us. The Reverend Rossie Brower, their father, was a Methodist minister, and the family lived across the street. When the girls were very young, Reverend Brower died. Unable to find work in Orange-burg to support her two daughters, the minister's widow, Henrietta, went north to New York to get work. Mama agreed to take care of Rossie and Eleanor, so they grew up with us like our sisters. Rossie was homecoming queen at Claflin University and later married Dr. Harlowe Caldwell, a dentist. Rossie and my wife, Bernice, both taught library science during their professional years at S.C. State University, and Rossie lived in Orange-burg until her recent passing. Eleanor died young while I was away in military service.

There were really eight children in our home, four girls and four boys, even though only six of us were actual blood brothers and sisters. Helen, Louise, Rossie, and Eleanor helped with the cooking and inside cleaning. Along with Mama, they washed clothes in the same tin tub we used for baths. Really dirty clothes were boiled in hot water; for that we had an iron pot in the yard that would be filled with water and fire heated. Then the girls would hang the clothes outside on a line to dry. The last stage of the laundry chore was ironing the clothes. Mama allowed none of her children to wear soiled clothes except when we got dirty playing outside.

Many families kept their own livestock and did slaughtering as they needed meat. We had hogs and chickens. In the winter Mama had a man come and butcher the hogs. This produced delicious hams and pork, but the part we most enjoyed was the cracklings made by roasting the skin. Today we get these "skins" from barbeque restaurants.

My brothers and I learned carpentry skills as we helped Papa make repairs on our house. He also taught us how to work safely with electrical wiring. Everything relating to our house and yard had to be kept clean, neat, repaired, and in order.

From our home alongside the railroad tracks, Mama illustrated the attitude she and Papa set for us about sharing what little we had with others. In those days hobos rode the rails from place to place. They somehow seemed to know where they could get food when they were hungry, and in the 1920s and 1930s there were many hungry people. Mama would always find a way to stretch the food we had to feed the hungry souls that appeared at our door. These men were sometimes black and sometimes white. It didn't matter with my family. A human in need was fed at our home. As I think back about it, I wonder why they didn't try to rob us or hurt us, but these vagrants must have known who would help them. I never saw Mama turn one away even if she had to cook for him.

When one of us children got sick, Mama had a homemade herbal medicine that was as bitter as you can imagine, but it would kill any kind of stomachache. Back then she would put herbs and roots in a jar and pour whiskey over them, and the remedy would be ready when needed. We wouldn't dare get into it unless we had a stomachache, though, because Mama would think we just wanted to drink that liquor. In the winter we would drink sassafras tea to head off flu and colds. All of us were also required to wear little bags of herbs around our necks to ward off illness. Sometimes we'd wear them so long they'd turn black, but Mama made us keep wearing them.

One time Mama got sick, and before she decided to call Dr. Seibels Remington Green, our family physician, a friend came by and suggested that she should try a whiskey cure. She brought a half-pint of whiskey and left it on the mantel in Mama's bedroom. Before anyone could move it the minister from our church came making one of his regular sick visits. When he left we thought Mama was going to die—not from her illness but from her embarrassment about the preacher seeing the whiskey bottle on the mantel.

Dr. Green, a black physician, was very popular with his black patients and was known as an excellent doctor. He lived on Treadwell Street and had two sons who became medical doctors. One was Dr. Carl Green, who I understand lives at Hilton Head. His brother was also well respected for his medical work, but he died young. They had a sister, Marilyn, who married Joe Bryant Epps, and they lived in Orangeburg. Another one of our black Orangeburg physicians was Dr. Monroe Crawford, who married Dr. Daniel Moorer's daughter, Allie. Dr. Crawford's son, Monroe Jr., became a medical doctor practicing surgery in Houston, Texas, and his son, George, was an attorney before his recent death.

Some of the other black families I remember our family having relationships with were the Bowmans, the Bryants, the Blassingames, and the Dantzlers on Dunton Street; the Fredericks, the Capers Robinsons, and the Thompsons on Goff Avenue; the Fordham-Smith-Robinson family on Boulevard; and the Thompsons, the Daniels, the Rowes (a medical doctor and his family), the Williamses, the Dashes, the Caldwells, the Moorers, and the Emblys on Treadwell Street. In addition, I can recall the Ben Baileys on Oak Street near our home, the Sultons, and the Carrion-Lewis family, as well as the Jarvis family, who lived in our neighborhood. We were allowed to associate only with people whom our mother considered of good character. They had to be church people to pass her muster. Money and social position were not concerns of hers, but principles definitely were.

Our family had been associated with Trinity United Methodist since its founding shortly after the Civil War. My grandfather Abram Middleton is said to have been one of the first pastors there. When the church was formed, it was located near where the Orangeburg County Courthouse stands today. That's where we attended church when I was a very young boy, but sometime in the 1920s construction on the new church building at the fork of Amelia Street and Boulevard was begun. Most of my boyhood I can remember going to services in temporary quarters at this location. In the early 1940s, while I was away serving in World War II, worship services were first held in the fine brick structure we still use today. The ministers at Trinity during my boyhood were the Reverend R. F. Freeman and, when Reverend Freeman died, the Reverend Robert F. Harrington. Reverend Harrington told the congregation on his first Sunday that he was the second "R.F." to minister at Trinity.

When my brothers and sisters and I were young, our friends, boys and girls, came to our house to play because we had a large family. Sometimes when we played baseball and it was a girl's time to bat, we would play "one old cat," which means that she would bat and then go out in the field in the hot sun to catch. Occasionally some white children who lived nearby would join our game. We never discussed the race issue. The use of profanity was prohibited. If anyone cursed out there in the field, Mama would break up the whole game.

Mama was a strict disciplinarian. I guess she'd had plenty of practice all those years of teaching school. As for my brothers and me, when one of us did something wrong, all of us would get a whipping. (She never whipped the girls.) I wondered why Mama would whip all of us even if only one did something wrong. Then I found out that's how she kept one of us checking up on the others. We got into most of our devilment when our parents went to prayer meeting and only we children were in the house. As soon as Mama got home and found something wrong, one of us would say, "Mama, I didn't do it." Then we'd all have to line up for whippings.

When school was out in the summers, from about the time I reached ten years of age, Mama would go to New York and do domestic work. Yes, she had a college degree *and* did domestic work. When Mama was away for those summers my big sister Helen, the oldest child, took charge of the home chores and family duties. Leaving Helen in charge took that burden off Papa so as not to interfere with his earning capacity. It was Helen's responsibility to keep all of us in line. Her authority came from Mama. If we didn't behave, she would report it to Mama. Then we'd have hell to pay.

My respect and friendship with Jewish people comes from the family for whom Mama worked up north, the Aaron Chases of New Rochelle, New York. My brother Phillip has reminded me that Mr. Chase was in the haberdashery or clothing business. They had several children and treated Mama as though she were a member of their family, sometimes even lending her money to help with our schooling. Mama worked up there only in the summers so she could be home when we were in school and make sure we progressed to her satisfaction. When she left New York to return south the Chases always sent along a barrel of hand-me-down clothes and shoes just in time for our back-to-school needs. Without this help my siblings and I would have had very little in the way of clothing. As glad as we were to have Mama back home, we were almost as glad to get the goodies from the Chases. There were four of us boys—Samuel Thaddeus, James Walter, Phillip Govan, and me. When the barrel of secondhand goodies arrived, the oldest boy had first choice of the male clothing. One time I remember I saw a reversible vest that I wanted, but James said, "Oh no, I want that!" So I had to let him wear it first. Later, after he had his chance at it, he let me wear it.

When Mama got up in age and no longer worked for the Chase family, they would stop by Orangeburg on their way to Florida and visit her. Orangeburg is on U.S. Highway 301, at that time the direct route from New York to Florida. That was before construction of Interstate 95, which now carries the bulk of the Florida–New York vehicle traffic and crosses Orangeburg County about twenty miles east of the city of Orangeburg at the Santee-Cooper lakes.

When the county fair arrived in Orangeburg once a year, the races were kept segregated by restricting black admissions to one or two days of the week. As a result of this restriction, blacks in the 1930s built our own fairgrounds off the present-day Ellis Avenue Extension. Fairs were held there until integration became a fact of life at the Orangeburg Fairgrounds, in the 1970s I think. At our black fairs we could relax without worry of some racial incident that might upset the town leaders and cause them to take retribution on the black community. The "colored fair," as it was called, had rides, games, exhibits, food, and horse races similar to those at the other fairgrounds. Agriculture was a large industry in Orangeburg County in those days, so there were major exhibits related to local fruits, vegetables, cotton, and other farm products.

While I was growing up, my family had contact with a few white families. The location of the railroad tracks by our house divided our neighborhood from a predominately white one on the other side of the tracks. We would shoot marbles with some of the white boys who came to our side of the tracks delivering the *Columbia Record* newspapers. They would let us ride their bicycles, as our parents could not afford bikes for us. I would volunteer to complete their route delivery of newspapers in the black neighborhood while my brothers engaged them in a match to try to win their superior-quality marbles. One of the boys was C. Walker Limehouse, who grew up to become an Orangeburg attorney and a business ally of mine. One of the Brailsford boys was also a paper carrier whose route came through our neighborhood.

Another white person who came into our neighborhood with regular deliveries to our home was the milkman from Verdery's Dairy. When our supply of milk from Verdery's ran out, we would be sent with a Jewel bucket to buy milk from the Atkinson family's cow. (Jewel was a brand of lard used for cooking. Mama bought it in large metal cans about two gallons in size. After we used all the lard, we would wash the can and use it for a milk or water pail.) The Atkinsons were one of the white families who lived in the neighborhood across the railroad tracks from our home. Today Dr. Eugene Atkinson, a descendant of this family, and I both belong to the Orangeburg Kiwanis Club.

Joseph C. Freeland was an engineer who worked for the Atlantic Coastline Railway. He and his wife, Lydia, had a house in this white neighborhood on Boulevard Street. After Mr. Freeland died in 1932, Mrs. Freeland asked Maxwell's Grocery to deliver as she did not drive. At that time I had a job delivering for Maxwell's in a little truck. Along with Maxwell's regular deliveryman, Mr. Counts, I would take groceries to the Freeland home. Maxwell had his employees wear white aprons over our street clothes to add a touch of professionalism. At the Freeland home I left the groceries in a chair on their screened back porch. Their daughter, Josephine Freeland Shuler, who is younger than I, still lives on that property. My grandmother Margaret Govan, who lived with us in her later years, was very friendly with the Wolfes, who lived across from the Freelands on our side of Boulevard Street.

The Sifly family, whose home was also in this area facing Boulevard, were devoted Methodists and attended church regularly. When the grapes in the arbor behind their house ripened we could smell them all over the neighborhood. On Wednesday evenings when they were attending prayer meetings, my brothers and a couple of our friends would climb the fence into their yard and help them "harvest" their scuppernong grapes. It was pitch dark when we got down on our hands and knees and filled our pockets to overflowing.

Alexander C. Lewis was a friend who participated in the "grape harvest." He was like a brother to us. His family attended Trinity United Methodist with our family. His mother, Annie C. Lewis, was one of Mama's closest friends. They lived between our house and town on Boulevard, near the Siflys' grape arbor. He and my brother Phillip went through school together and served in the same army engineering unit during World War II. Alex and I were in the same church together and remained lifelong friends until he passed several years ago.

I was recalling some of these white families residing near our home, and it reminded me that Mama and Papa never discussed race with us.

They set the example by their actions. When the occasions arose they dealt with white people in the same way they did anyone else. Nothing was ever said about a person being black or white in our home. Although I didn't know it as a young child, looking back I can now see that in this small South Carolina town we lived a parallel existence with the whites who also called Orangeburg home—same location but different worlds.

My family subscribed to a newspaper called the *Grit*. We always had a newspaper coming into our home. Papa would come home from work and read to Mama about what was going on while she was cooking dinner. I delivered the *Grit*. It was a weekly paper that was started in 1882 in Williamsport, Pennsylvania, and specialized in small-town distribution mostly by boys. The positive tone insisted on by its owner, Dietrick Lamade, helped parlay the *Grit* into one of America's biggest and most enduring publications. Total circulation hit 1.5 million in 1969, and it is still published in 2007 in magazine form every other month. We would sit around the table listening to Papa read the paper as we ate.

Oh how we ate! Mama cooked sumptuous, made-from-scratch food. Why do we remember our mothers' dinners as being the best of our lives? I don't have the answer to that unless it's because as children we have such ravenous appetites, especially boys. I distinctly remember the bread rolls Mama made. I could eat a dozen at a time. As she pulled a pan of hot ones from the oven, she brushed them with melted butter and put sugar on the top. Sometimes she made them for church functions too.

At the Middleton home Sunday was a special day. It was completely given over to worship and family. In the morning Papa would read from the Bible, and we'd have devotions before going to church. There was absolutely no work done on the Sabbath other than that related to preparing our food or cleaning up following the meal. Sunday after church was the occasion for our special meal of the week. The menu would often include baked chicken, ham, macaroni and cheese, collard greens, tomatoes, butter beans, carrots, green salad, homemade yeast rolls, gelatin, or ice cream. We had a hand-cranked ice-cream churn that we used to produce our own at home.

Family dinners at the Middletons on Sundays also served as occasions for etiquette training for us children. Mama would use her nicest tablecloth. She taught the girls the proper placement of the tableware, including the china, flatware, glasses, and serving pieces. She had a special set of flatware used only for Sunday dinners and other special meals, such as when the preacher and his wife were dining with our family. We were taught the correct use of our utensils and table manners. All our meals began with Papa saying the blessing of thanks.

During the weekdays meals were less formal, and we didn't always eat at the same time because of school and work schedules. Mama had her system for these meals too. The rule was when you came in to eat you asked who hadn't eaten yet. If there were others coming to eat after you, it was mandatory that ample food be left for those remaining.

Recently my brother Phillip and I were discussing Mama's family dinners. Phillip said he believes that the way she made those dinners so special for us was a large factor in our having such a healthy concept of self-worth. It was a subconscious thing. Witnessing the care Mama put into making those Sabbath dinners a family celebration each week told us that our satisfaction was worth all that effort. They were distinctive enough to give us the feeling that we were unique and deserving of her efforts. From being in white families' homes when we were doing chores for them, we knew what a nice dining room was like; when we saw their well-dressed tables, we knew that we were in this league. I think Phillip is right: the standards Mama set regularly in our family dining experiences helped me know who I am.

We knew our family members who lived in places other than Orangeburg too. Some, like many blacks in the early 1920s, had fled the South to find work in the North. Some of them lived in New York, and they would visit us. Mama used to tell us about Papa's sisters and brothers living in New York near each other or in the same building, as I recall. They had always been a close family. Papa stayed in the South but did not get as much education as Mama because he had that deathbed agreement with Granddaddy to educate his brothers and sisters and went to work to do this.

Families can be our best allies and our worst enemies all at the same time. The fact that my grandfather Abram Middleton did not leave a will came back to work a hardship on our family. He left Papa in charge of property he had purchased just after the Civil War and "gave" him the house on Clark Street where we lived. Papa managed the properties and, I believe, collected some meager rent moneys to offset maintenance expenses partially.

However, Granddaddy's other heirs decided they wanted their portion of his estate. Since my grandfather had children by two wives, there were about twenty children, grands, and other descendants who brought suit against Papa to recover part of the estate. Papa had no choice but to get a lawyer to reply. It appears that the courts decided Papa should get credit for the work and materials he had put into the properties entrusted to him and then ordered the assets sold and divided proportionately. Papa was able to take his share of the inheritance and the credits for maintenance and borrow the remainder to purchase the Clark Street house. Forget the education he gave up to ensure that others received one; the judge obviously didn't consider that if he even knew about it. Although that was the year before I was born, I remember the tight financial times we experienced as a result. It was one of life's lasting lessons to me about putting agreements in writing.

Papa was such an excellent craftsman that many building contractors came to seek his counsel about their projects. They would come to him on Saturday, and I would see him drawing out plans for these educated people who had been to school. He would explain how to work out difficulties in their plans and then would sketch ideas out and wouldn't charge them. I could not understand at that time why he didn't charge them. Today we're still enjoying the goodwill resulting from what he did to help people. He built up so much rapport with people that their descendants are still doing favors for us. One of the contractors was a Mr. Richardson who lived on Oak Street in the city of Orangeburg. Another was Mr. Robert Spigner on Dixon Street, who did a lot of remodeling work for whites on their homes. Another whose name I can't recall lived just south of the Edisto River on the main highway.

All my brothers and I went into the same line of work, real estate. My brothers James and Phillip were contractors in Los Angeles, California, before they retired. My oldest brother, Sam, an educator, taught carpentry in the public schools of South Carolina early in his career. I've been in the real estate brokerage business for about fifty years. Today my son, Kenny, is in the business too.

It's ironic to me that real estate, an occupation initiated by my grandfather when he was a slave, is the same one by which we earn our living today. People didn't call it "real estate" during slave times, but as a carpenter Granddaddy repaired and built buildings. He even managed to find a way to acquire property though it was illegal for slaves to own real estate. Since his first wife was a free woman, they simply purchased the property in her name. A big part of our lives and history as a black family has been turning adversity around to positive results. From the horribly negative situation of slavery that our ancestors were forced into when they came to America, succeeding generations of Middletons have managed to make good lives for ourselves.

2

Impressions

Mama Made Us Hustle

In addition to our schoolwork and home chores, as my brothers and I entered our teenage years, we began to do yard work and odd jobs around Orangeburg for some of the white families. My initiation into the world of outside work was through my oldest brother, Sam. Sam was the so-called houseboy for the H. A. Wright family. Mr. Wright was the cashier (head teller) at Planters Bank. Sam began working for the Wrights when he was about twelve years old. The duties consisted mainly of yard work but also included carrying coal into the furnace room of the house. After Sam completed the eleventh grade, he spent the summer in New York with one of our aunts. I worked in his place at the Wrights', who lived at 17 Lovell Street. That was within walking distance of our house beyond State College, and of course we walked everywhere we went.

The Wright house was of modest size. It contained a dining room, a living room, a kitchen, three bedrooms, and a bath, and there was a large porch around the entire house. It was well furnished, not impressively but completely. Mr. Wright had one daughter, Margaret. Sam told me that the Wannamaker family helped her get a scholarship to Duke University. She was educated there and ultimately became a librarian working for the State of South Carolina, according to Sam.

When we worked out in the community we were instructed to bring our earnings home to our parents, especially to Mama. This money would help supplement our family's needs between Papa's paychecks. We brought her all our earnings through the time we were in high school. She could stretch money and was an excellent manager. She would give back to us what she thought we needed to have. Sometimes she would take the money to the store when she shopped on weekends and buy us candy, such as silver bells, licorice, and kisses. Another reason Mama had for making us turn our money over to her was to make sure that none of it had been ill-gotten. When my brothers and I later worked together in a small business, Sam, James, and Phillip always complimented me on my money-management skills. I definitely learned those from Mama.

My next job outside our home was working for Robert H. Jennings Jr., the mayor of Orangeburg. He and his family lived on Broughton Street in a house that's still occupied today, though by an unrelated family. Because Mr. Wright was impressed with my work he recommended me to Mayor Jennings. My main responsibility at the Jennings home was to cut the yard and trim the hedges. Their hedges were headquarters for wasp nests. They grew thick, and you could not see into the growth. As I was clipping, the tip of the shears would catch an unseen nest of the critters and they would fly out and sting me. After a couple of summers I'd seen all the wasps I cared to meet. I left word for Mr. Jennings with their cook that I was quitting. When I went back on the weekend to collect my money for the work I'd done, Mr. Jennings asked, "Earl, why are you quitting?" Not wanting to offend him, I fibbed by saying, "Mama thinks I need to spend more time on my schoolwork." With that I knew he wouldn't try to persuade me to continue.

Other jobs I had growing up included farm work such as picking cotton, stripping fodder, and driving a farm truck. Anyone could pick cotton; no training was necessary. When a farmer needed cotton pickers, he sent a truck to town to pick up people willing to do the work. We were paid by the weight of cotton harvested, so it behooved us to gather as much as possible—or find a way for it to be heavier. This was accomplished by peeing in the cotton, getting it slightly wet and adding to its weight. When the boss man came back and weighed the cotton, the pickers were a little better off.

Of course, we were not allowed to let our outside work interfere with school in any way. We went to school at Claflin. I never did go to any school but Claflin, which was begun by the Methodist Episcopal Church in 1869 and continues to be sponsored by the United Methodist Church. The Methodist Episcopal Church split in the 1840s over the issue of slavery. The proslavery churches became Methodist Episcopal–South. Our ancestors were trained by white Methodist Episcopal missionaries who moved to South Carolina from the Northeast during the Civil War. The Reverend Timothy Willard Lewis and the Reverend Alonzo Webster were two of these men. Because whites dominated the hierarchy of the Methodist Episcopal Church, some blacks became dissatisfied. They broke off and started joining the national African Methodist Episcopal Church, which was established in Philadelphia in 1816 with Richard Allen as its first bishop.

Our family saw the merit of remaining with the Methodist Episcopal Church, which became the United Methodist Church in the 1970s. Claflin provided elementary school, high school, and college. There was not a public high school that blacks in Orangeburg could go to until 1937, so the importance of Claflin to the Middleton family was overwhelming. In a family with six children to get through school, not only did we have to work hard but we also had to be clever in figuring how we could pay for school. Mama's work laundering the tablecloths for Claflin helped in that regard. Then my older brothers hit on a money-earning idea that went a long way toward covering our educational expenses.

Claflin was in need of structures to house faculty members. During the summer of 1940 James, Phillip, and I constructed a house that is now used as the campus infirmary. Basically Phillip came up with the idea and implemented it through a contract with Claflin. He recruited James and me as his employees, and Papa served as his expert consultant. The college needed this house to replace one on the campus that had burned. It became the home for the dean of the college and his wife, Mr. and Mrs. Henry Pearson. The college gave us credit for this work against our tuition and fees. Claflin did similar things to make education possible for other students too. Today Claflin University continues to do everything it can to help students who need financial aid. Members of the Middleton family continue our relationship with Claflin. In 2000 Phillip's grandson, Nye Tucker III, received his undergraduate degree at Claflin. My son, Kenny, presently serves on the board of trustees there.

Even though Mama and Papa had never owned a car by the time I got to college, I had somehow managed to learn to drive trucks and automobiles—and I was a good driver. Joseph B. Randolph from Pass Christian, Mississippi, served as president of Claflin College from 1922 until 1945, the entire time I was there in school. When he got ready to take a trip to Mississippi from Orangeburg, he needed a driver for his car; in fact, he needed two drivers because Pass Christian is more than a day's trip. James Hall (now deceased) and I were chosen by President Randolph for the coveted work. The president also had a brother in New Jersey, an attorney, he'd visit. In addition there were trips related to college business closer to home. For instance, when the Claflin College choir was scheduled to perform at a Methodist church in Columbia, President Randolph needed to be there to introduce them, so we drove him there and back. We sometimes drove faculty members and students on trips at the president's request. For example, we drove Miss Marie Martin, an English professor, and Miss Harvey Lee Ward, a librarian, on trips. Although these trips were infrequent, my work as a driver was important to the college and to me personally in terms of the tuition credit I received.

Working for a shoemaker, Johnny Oliver, was another work experience for me during my college years. In the beginning I would shine the shoes and boots at his shop on the Railroad Corner. Then I graduated to putting on half-soles and heels. The leather for the soles came in a large sheet, and we would cut them to fit and stitch them with a special machine. Store-bought shoes were not as readily available then as they are today. Most shoes and boots were made of leather, and besides naturally lasting a long time, their life could be stretched even more with new half-soles and heels.

Another "hustle" my brother Phillip and I had was barbering. We gave haircuts and shaves in a small space beside Lyon's Grocery Store on Goff Avenue near Claflin University. Papa's brother John Middleton was a barber at the well-known Herndon's Barber Shop in Atlanta. He influenced me to learn this skill, and I still have his barber tools, which I inherited from him.

The building that housed Lyon's Store has since been torn down. It was an old frame structure with a *V* tin roof. Mr. Lyons sold groceries downstairs and used the upstairs to store his merchandise. A stairway provided access to the upstairs storage area. He sold cheese from a large round block, which was contained on a holder with a built-in knife. If a customer wished to purchase five cents' worth of cheese he would lift the handle one notch; for ten cents' worth the handle was lifted two notches. Then the blade would cut off that amount of cheese. Likewise bacon came in a slab and was sliced by hand to the customers' orders.

Off on one side adjoining the store Mr. Lyons had a little separate shop that was of frame construction with a flat tin roof. I had my one-chair barbershop in there. This space I rented from Mr. Lyons for about fifty cents a month. One of my regular customers was Mr. Glover, an older man who owned a mom-and-pop, country-style grocery store at the corner of

Goff and Buckley streets, about two blocks from my barbershop. After he closed his store on Saturday evenings, he would come in for a weekly shave and haircut. He was my last customer of the day. There were two things on my mind as I worked on Mr. Glover. Number one: I wanted to do a good job on him because he appreciated the service, told other men about my work, and was a good tipper. Number two: I wanted to finish in time to make it to the 10:45 P.M. movie at the Carolina Theater on Middleton Street, in the same building where Stevenson Auditorium and Orangeburg City Hall are housed today.

When Mr. Glover came to my shop he was tired. First I would cut his hair, and by the time I finished he would be relaxed enough to go to sleep in my barber's chair. He had an extremely tough beard, and, since I was using a straight razor, I had to be very careful not to cut him. In fact his beard was so tough that, while he was asleep, I would run across the street and borrow a safety razor from my friend Claflin Kennerly. Then I would run back over to my shop and finish Mr. Glover's beard. He would get up and pay me eighty-five cents. Sometimes I would get my brother Phillip to help with Mr. Glover's shave.

Ordinarily I charged fifteen cents for haircuts and ten cents for shaves. Since I worked at this endeavor only on Saturdays, I could do probably fifteen haircuts and some shaves a week. I do remember that I grossed between three dollars and ten dollars each Saturday. Supplies such as soap, lather, and towels had to be paid for as well as rent. After deducting those the net was a healthy profit. In addition to honing my barbering skills and learning how to run a profitable business, I also had extra money to carry home to Mama to help pay for a college education for all her children. Barbering and driving the president of Claflin were jobs I did intermittently during my late high school and college years.

At the end of the summer of 1940 James, Phillip, and I felt successful after completing the house on the Claflin campus. As a result one of my next work endeavors involved a more ambitious business venture with them. We decided to open a café on the Railroad Corner near the colleges across from the Southern Railway train station. Our café was known as the Silver Grill. We had an eating bar that would seat about ten—three booths, and three tables. We obtained our tableware and cooking utensils from Ferse's five-and-dime. My brothers and I had done yard work around town for years and had each saved a little money. We used this as the investment to open our restaurant. Even at that we operated on a shoestring, to say the least.

An example of our modus operandi was reflected in our menu. At this time America was still feeling the effects of the Great Depression. The failure of the cotton economy had deepened financial suffering in the South. The average person had little available cash, and we were no exception. We included many items on our menu that an ordinary restaurant could not afford to have on hand—and we didn't keep those items on hand either. Here's how it worked. A man would come in and order a steak dinner. Knowing we had no beef in the refrigerator, I would disappear to the back kitchen area as though preparing his order. Quickly I'd duck into the meat market next to Maxwell's store, purchase one steak, and be back in our kitchen before he knew I was gone. Then I'd head back to the front, where I'd ask, "Oh, how do you like your steak prepared, sir?" By the time he answered medium, well done, or rare I'd have the grill heated and could pop the steak right on.

We had little quarter machines at the Silver Grill, similar to piggy banks, and we used them to start saving money. When the amount in a machine got to be between seven and ten dollars, a person could take it out and put it in his or her bank. We did not have any bank accounts. This is the way we accumulated money to buy an appliance or a piece of equipment. If we knew we were going to need to buy a cooler, then we would start saving quarters.

James, Phillip, and I rotated working at our Silver Grill, and we ran a very respected business for high school and college students. The business operated for several years before the three of us went into military service. Sam was working as a school principal, but our grill was doing so well he decided to switch over to running the restaurant. Then in 1944, when Sam too went into the armed services, we were forced to sell the café.

An account of our businesses was written by Dr. Horace Fitchett, a Claflin history professor, and published in the *Negro History Bulletin* in 1944 while my brothers and I were serving our country. A sequential listing of these jobs shows that increased skills were required as we moved up the job ladder from picking cotton to, say, repairing shoes or chauffeuring. Yet we kept at it long enough to ensure that all the children in our family were able to earn four-year college degrees during the Great Depression. We were taught how to work to better our lives.

White-Hooded Terrorists

While I was in the midst of composing this book, terrorists commandeered U.S. commercial airliners on September 11, 2001, crashing two of

them into the twin World Trade Center towers in New York City, crashing another into the Pentagon in Washington, and causing another to
crash in Pennsylvania. As a result some three thousand American and foreign civilians were killed. All Americans were thrown into a state of shock
that this could happen inside our country. As I reflected on these horrendous tragedies I came to realize that blacks in America have lived with terrorism inside our borders for centuries. For example, between 1859 and
1959 there were five thousand lynchings of blacks in America. My first
exposure to terrorism at home came when I was a youngster.

I was about twelve or thirteen years old when I learned there was separate racial seating in the movie houses here in Orangeburg. Blacks were
required to sit in the balcony; we called it the "buzzard's roost." We liked
to go and see a Tom Mix or similar movie. One day we got permission
from my parents to attend a late afternoon movie, probably on Russell
Street downtown. I saw my father sitting on the front porch of our Clark
Street home by himself. Earlier, either that day or that week, there had
been an announcement in the local newspaper that the Ku Klux Klan was
to march that night. I didn't think much about it because my family had
never been engaged in anything that would cause us to be concerned. We
knew we had a good family and thought our parents were strong enough
to protect us from anything. As Papa sat on the front porch I walked out
there to say something to him. He had a strange look on his face that I
had never before seen. He was sitting very quietly. I asked him something
about the newspaper article on the Ku Klux Klan march planned for the
outskirts of the city of Orangeburg, which would include the area where
we were living at the time. Papa didn't reply to my curiosity.

A lot of black people were afraid because we never had any good experiences when things like that happened. Fortunately, when the white-
hooded bullies came by that night, there was no violence. We watched
from our darkened windows as they passed between our home and the
railroad tracks. Each of them was carrying some kind of light that looked
like a torch. When they got to the end of their journey they retraced their
route and marched by our house again. I guess the purpose of their march
that evening was to remind black people that members of the Klan and
their white sympathizers were in control and to give us the message that
if we didn't keep "our place," violence would result. Beginning in the
1860s, this kind of terrorism was imposed on blacks in America for more
than a hundred years.

As I have said, we never did discuss race in our house. I don't know why; possibly it was because of my parents' training or their religious leanings. Maybe they used this method of silence to protect us as young children from the psychological damage we might suffer if we knew about the white-imposed system of racial segregation in our country. My brothers and sisters and I didn't know much about discrimination at that point in our lives. Our parents were well trained, and so were we. We were as well dressed as poor people could be at that time. We lived in our area of the city, and the whites lived in theirs. Even when we shot marbles with the white newspaper-delivery boys the subject of segregation did not come up, and we seldom associated socially with other whites. We accepted the fact that whites were downstairs and we were in the balcony at the theater because the law said that's the way it had to be. Since Claflin was a private school we had few contacts with whites there.

Those relationships that my family did have with whites seemed to be positive to the extent that the system of racial segregation allowed in those days. The "system" was the problem. Individuals were our friends; the system was the obstacle preventing black people from being viewed as equal human beings. It can be argued that whites controlled the system, which is true, and that has long been the dilemma for the black minority.

My parents didn't specifically talk about race issues. Mama and Papa were not militant in their attitudes or actions. They taught us by their example, being considerate to all people. We did yard work for the white people who wanted us to and paid us for it, and that was our only contact with them. We didn't *want* to go anywhere we were unwanted.

That afternoon on the front porch, when I saw that strange look on Papa's face after I asked him about the Klan, I had my first exposure to the fact that some things happening in our lives and in the country were related to the color of my skin and racial features. After all these years, even though I never figured out his exact thinking, I knew he was in a quandary. He was terrified. He expressed his concern by his silence, and that made an impression on me.

Today it is easy to look back and wonder why we accepted being terrorized, segregated, denied equal access to the same facilities as whites, and worse. Mama and Papa protected us by being stoic. This was generally what most black Americans did then. In hindsight one could ask why they weren't militant enough to go against the system of racial segregation. Some blacks did go against the system, and sometimes they paid with their lives. When there was enough of a critical mass of opposition built up against the system, then positive change was brought about.

During my childhood there were many black people still living who remembered when slavery was legal in our country. In America slavery was based on color and race. (Oh yes, I realize there were black slave owners too, and they contributed to the wrongdoing, no question. However, their numbers were so minuscule in the scheme of things that they hadn't the power to effect any change in the system even if they wanted to.) Because whites had historically been in control of the legal system in our country, blacks knew that if we tried to use that route the chances of success were practically nil. My parents had enough sense to know that if they taught their family Christian values and saw that we were educated, we would survive and thrive regardless of how much the system was against us as black people.

Special Neighbors and a Role Model

Although we had no telephone at our home, we sometimes used that of a neighboring family, the Alonzo Bryants, about a block away. This is how I met my future wife, Anna Bernice Bryant (known as Bernice). Her maternal grandfather, the Reverend C. H. Dangerfield, was a Methodist minister from Charleston. Bernice's family had longtime ties to Claflin University just as the Middletons did. Her mother, Gertrude Dangerfield Bryant, was principal of the Business College in the early 1920s and later worked in the university president's office. Two of Bernice's uncles graduated with college degrees from Claflin; one went on to become a medical doctor, and the other became a dentist.

Almost certainly named for the first president of Claflin, Bernice's father, Alonzo Webster Bryant, earned his bachelor's degree in industrial arts. He was a teacher at Claflin and later in Darlington County, South Carolina. His expertise was in an interesting area of manual arts that is virtually unknown today. He taught "sloyd," a system of manual training that originated in Sweden. It is based on the use of hand tools in wood carving and joining. In the early part of the twentieth century a lot of furniture was still made by hand. Sloyd was a very important school subject, especially for young men, because mastery of it enabled one to achieve a highly sought after skill. Of course, after World War II, when machinery made mass production possible, handmade furniture became obsolete and sloyd was dropped from school curricula.

Bernice and her brother, Alonzo Jr., nicknamed "Butch," both received their education at Claflin from the first grade through college graduation. Butch became an architect and lives in California.

Although Bernice is four years younger than me, by the time we were in high school she was at the same grade level I was. Because she was such a good student and was able to learn the lessons more quickly than the average student, she skipped several grades to catch up to my class. She was an exceptional student all through elementary school, college, and graduate school, eventually becoming a librarian and a college professor. In fact Bernice is one of the main reasons I got through school; she helped me in my school work.

During my college years Mama had a job washing and ironing the linens for Claflin's dining hall. After she finished, my brothers and I had to deliver them in the wheelbarrow back to the campus. It was very embarrassing for me to have my girlfriends see me rolling the wheelbarrow with the linens on it back to the dining hall. Some of the other guys had cars on campus, and the girls liked that. I was ashamed for them to see me without a car. Even so delivering those linens was one of the jobs Mama required us to do. She had her financial plan for making sure we all got through school, and that laundry job was part of it.

Sometime during my student years I first became interested in politics. All four years in college I was elected as class president. When I was in school, I heard about I. S. Leevy, a successful businessman from Camden, South Carolina. He had migrated to Columbia and had a prosperous funeral business and owned land. He was free to pursue politics because, with his own business, he did not have to ask anyone if he could take time off from work. He was my idol, and I would try to hang around him as much as possible. He went all over the state and spoke about what blacks needed to do to be successful. I'll never forget his telling us that most blacks were either too poor or too disinterested to go where the information was. He inspired me to be a businessman because that gave you advantages you didn't have as an employee.

Through I. S. Leevy, I was put in touch with Modjeska Simkins, one of the founders of Victory Savings Bank in Columbia. This lady was a heroine to many people. As well as being a businesswoman, she also was a dedicated activist for black peoples' rights.

I. S. Leevy influenced me to begin working with the Republican Party. At that time we as black people in the South could not join the Democratic

Party, but we were still welcomed by the Republicans. In the 1930s, 1940s, and 1950s the Democratic Party in the South was still controlled by leaders with an antiblack agenda. Politicians such as "Cotton" Ed Smith and James Byrnes in South Carolina and Eugene Talmadge in Georgia did not hide their biases.

The president of North Carolina Mutual Life Insurance Company in Durham, North Carolina, was another successful businessman to whom I was exposed at an impressionable age. He spoke to us in chapel at Claflin College. Even so, that onetime exposure did not influence me to the extent that my repeated contacts with the esteemed I. S. Leevy did.

The Reverend Abram Middleton, Earl Middleton's grandfather. This photograph, which hung over the mantel in Samuel E. Middleton's home at 638 Clark Street in Orangeburg, was damaged when the roof leaked during the Depression years. Collection of the author

*Samuel Edgar Middleton,
Earl Middleton's father,
in later years on the steps
of his Clark Street home.
Collection of the author*

*Ella Govan Middleton,
Earl Middleton's mother,
standing by the kitchen
steps of the family's Clark
Street home, circa 1931.
Photograph courtesy of
Pauline Mansfield*

*Alonzo Webster Bryant Sr.,
father of Bernice Bryant
(Mrs. Earl Middleton),
circa 1930. Collection of
the author*

*Gertrude Dangerfield Bryant
(Mrs. Alonzo Webster
Bryant Sr.), mother of
Bernice Bryant Middleton,
circa 1945. Collection of
the author*

Alonzo W. "Butch" Bryant Jr. and his sister, Bernice Bryant, circa 1930. Collection of the author

Seven-room bungalow constructed by the Middleton brothers—James, Phillip, and Earl—under the direction of their father, Samuel E. Middleton, in the summer of 1940 for use as Claflin faculty housing. Moved from another part of campus to Goff Avenue, it now serves as the university infirmary. Photograph by Cecil Williams

Ella Govan Middleton,
circa 1960. Collection
of the author

Earl Middleton in his
Tuskegee Airman cadet
uniform, March 1942.
Photograph by P. H. Polk,
Tuskegee, Alabama

The Fourth Aviation Squadron at Maxwell Air Force Base, Alabama, circa 1943. Leading the troops is Capt. Morton B. Howell of Nashville, Tennessee. Cpl. Earl Middleton is carrying the guidon, just behind and to the right of Captain Howell. Photograph by Lt. Agnew Fisher, courtesy of the late Morton B. Howell

A Boeing/Stearman PT-17 "Kaydet," the same make and model as the plane in which Earl Middleton and other Tuskegee Airmen cadets trained. Photograph by Buck Wyndam, from http://warbirdalley.com/pt17, downloaded August 5, 2006

*Earl Middleton and Bernice
Bryant on May 29, 1944,
the day on which she
received her library science
degree from Atlanta University. Collection of the author*

*Earl Middleton in his battle gear
on Ie Shima, 1945. Collection of
the author*

Butch Bryant in his military uniform, circa 1944. Collection of the author

One of two Japanese "Betty Bombers" landing at Ie Shima on August 17, 1945, with the surrender envoy. Photograph by William Hurley

Part Two

Young Manhood

3

Working for My White Uncle

During my senior year at Claflin College, Pearl Harbor was attacked by Japanese warplanes on December 7, 1941. I knew I would go into the military. Right after Christmas I decided that, rather than waiting to be drafted, I'd volunteer and try to get into the U.S. Army Air Corps. At that time I'd heard that army soldiers who were drafted into the service were receiving salaries of $21 a month. I'd also been told that being accepted into the newly initiated training program for black pilots that was under way at Tuskegee Army Air Field in Alabama would bring a monthly salary of more than $275 gross. In that program I'd also be in training to become an officer, which was much more prestigious.

The details about exactly when and how I volunteered are gone from my mind, but it was all done in Orangeburg. The first time I left town was when I was called to report to Owens Field in Columbia, South Carolina, for a screening interview. I made the hour-plus drive to Columbia in my older brother Sam's used black Ford. I had my driver's license because I had already been driving the president of Claflin for several years. Before that day I'd never had any contact with military officials, so I wasn't sure what to expect.

Owens Field was a private airport. There's always been a question in my mind as to why the military was using Owens Field to conduct interviews. It was an open airfield with no gate or guards. According to the *State* newspaper, the airport was originally owned by aviation pioneers Orville and Wilbur Wright. Glenn Curtiss, Amelia Earhart, and President Franklin D. Roosevelt are said to have landed there. As instructed, I reported to the main headquarters building and was escorted to a room

with folding chairs and tables. In about forty-five minutes three army officers arrived and introduced themselves. I don't recall their names or ranks.

I was seated at a long table across from the three white officers, who
were very polite and respectful. They asked me only three questions. The
first question was "Who is Marian Anderson?" I replied, "She is a nation-
ally known vocalist." They made no remarks relating to my answer but
went directly to the next question, which was "Who is Joe Louis?" To that
question I answered, "He is a championship boxer." Again they gave no
reaction to my reply. The third question they put to me was "Who is
George Washington Carver?" I answered, "An outstanding scientist in
Alabama." At that point they looked at each other, and one of them said,
"You'll be hearing something from us." Then I was dismissed. Those were
the only questions I was asked. That was basically the extent of the interview, which lasted about ten minutes from start to finish. It was unbelievable to me that they would ask me questions along those lines.

Now I must say that the word had gotten out that I was planning to
go into the training program for black pilots at Tuskegee, and as a result
a lot of the girls at Claflin wanted to date me. The fact that I had been on
the football team and had served as class president for four years enhanced the situation. However, by this time Bernice Bryant had the inside
track in that regard.

The War Department wrote that I was accepted into the program. I
was instructed to report to Hawthorne Air Base in Orangeburg to be
sworn into the Army Air Corps training program. Hawthorne was constructed about three miles south on the outskirts of Orangeburg after
World War II started as a location for training Allied pilots for combat
missions. This is the property where a retirement community, the Oaks, is
now located. I remember it was on a clear day that I drove Sam's car out
Rowesville Road to the base. After being sworn in, I once again went back
to classes at Claflin to await my orders from the Army Air Corps.

The president of Claflin University talked to the entire student body
during chapel and told them I'd been selected by the War Department.
Everyone was happy for me, and it was a tribute to Claflin University for
one of its students to volunteer and be chosen for this new pilot training
program. My elation over my selection was about much more than any
personal popularity I might have had with my peer group. On the campus and in our family's circle of friends it was seen as a victory for black
Americans, and a local person had become the hero.

Within a few weeks I received orders to report to Tuskegee Army Air
Field. The War Department had enclosed a first-class train ticket from

Orangeburg to Cheehaw, Alabama, the passenger train depot nearest to Tuskegee.

Train to Tuskegee

On the appointed day I packed a small bag and walked to the Coastline Railway Station in Orangeburg to begin my journey. Today the station is in the exact same location, although it is no longer used for passengers, and now the name is Seaboard Coastline Railway. Upon arriving at the station I presented my ticket to the railway official. He studied it carefully, and by his countenance I knew that something was wrong. He said to me, "You can't get on this train here." At that point I understood that the problem he had was with the color of my skin. In the early 1940s there were in effect so-called Jim Crow laws in the southern states, including South Carolina. These laws basically barred blacks from equal access in public accommodations. On trains blacks always rode in a designated area of a coach-class car just behind the engine. Next was a mail car and then the first-class, all-whites car. The fact that I had a first-class ticket from the War Department was a problem for him because only whites were in the first-class cars and he was not allowed to assign me a seat with whites.

After being refused boarding I returned, once again, to classes at Claflin University. About a week later I was summoned to the president's office to receive a phone call from the War Department. I was informed that I was absent without official leave from the army and was going to be arrested because I had not shown up at Tuskegee as ordered. At that point I explained to the officer on the phone that I had not been allowed to board the train in Orangeburg. He told me the War Department would straighten that out. In a few days another ticket came. On February 23, 1942, I went back to the Coastline Railway Station in Orangeburg. I had just turned twenty-three years old.

What happened this time was amazing. When the train arrived from the main station in Florence, South Carolina, an empty first-class coach had been added to the train just to accommodate me! I rode all the way to Atlanta in that coach *alone*. I'm sure the expense the War Department incurred for that special car was considerable. This was a tangible example to me of the great costs incurred by the taxpayers to keep the races separated. It was almost unimaginable to me that anyone would go to these lengths and this kind of expense to perpetuate segregation.

In Atlanta I had to change trains. The train I was to connect with was carrying nothing but first-class Pullman coaches. It was out of Greenville-Spartanburg, South Carolina, and was going on into Alabama. I fetched my little bag and walked across the depot to the other station. I wasn't worried about anything!

When I arrived the train was in the station. I walked up to a white conductor on the designated platform and showed him my ticket. He told me I couldn't get on that train. As I tried to explain my situation to him another conductor came over and asked, "What's the problem?" The first conductor replied, "This nigger's trying to get on the train!" The second one told him, "You can't do that anymore," meaning that he couldn't keep me off the train. With that the first conductor spoke angrily to me, "Get on there and take number three." His tone didn't make any difference to me. I was supposed to get on the train. His intended insult didn't hurt my feelings. *I knew who I was,* and there was nothing he could say that would change that.

This car was a Pullman with individual compartments. I boarded and took number three. When it was time the train pulled off. I had a small boothlike compartment with a bed and curtains to pull for privacy on the aisle side. I had never seen anything like that before. On the opposite side were windows overlooking the landscape as it whizzed past. The train ride enhanced the feelings of pride and anticipation inside me as I contemplated the endeavor ahead of training to become an army pilot to serve my country. It appeared that finally black men would be given the opportunity to fight for America on an equal footing with whites.

My thoughts were interrupted as a white conductor came through the train taking tickets. Just behind him was a black porter sweeping up cigar and cigarette butts. He had on a rail porter's uniform, including the distinctive pillbox-shaped hat of the era. When the porter saw me, another black man, I thought he was going to turn white with shock. He didn't know what had happened that they would allow a black man to ride in a private Pullman compartment.

At this point the porter bent over as though something were wrong with his shoe in order to stall for time. Pretending to tie his shoelaces, while all the time keeping an eye on me, he allowed the conductor to get ahead of him enough to be out of sight. He was afraid that if he were seen talking with me he would risk losing his position. Being a railroad porter in those days was a coveted "big-time" job for a black man.

After the conductor went through our car the porter came running back to me and whispered, "Where are you going?" He also inquired as to where I was from. I told him, "I'm going down to Tuskegee, coming out of South Carolina." He asked, "Why you going down there?" I replied, "I'm going there to fly." Then he told me, "Some black fella back there about five coaches is going down there too. You want to meet him?" I told him I did and then left my little bag in my compartment and went back through several cars to meet this other black man. His name was Williams, and I never will forget him. He was from New York. I asked him how he had managed to be on that train, and his reply was, "The NAACP put hell on the War Department and got me in." We talked awhile, and then I went on back to my compartment.

It got lonesome for me in that compartment by myself. In order to stretch my legs I decided to walk through the regular passenger coach. During my "outing" I ran into a friend's sister from Orangeburg, Valeria Howard (now Staley). She was on her way to a Talladega school. At that time black families often sent their children out of town for secondary school in search of a more quality educational experience.

To begin the account of my experience at Tuskegee I will relate a brief history of the airmen from the inscription on a statue at the U.S. Air Force Academy in Colorado Springs, Colorado:

THE TUSKEGEE EXPERIMENT

The original Tuskegee Airmen evolved during World War II at a small Army airfield near Tuskegee, Alabama in what was called the "Tuskegee Experiment." The experiment involved the training of black pilots and ground support personnel to form the 99th Pursuit Squadron. This squadron was later joined by the 100th, 301st, and 302nd Squadrons forming the 332nd Fighter Group. They courageously flew combat in the P-40, P-39, P-47, and P-51 aircraft, distinguishing themselves while flying over 1500 missions, and never losing an escorted bomber to enemy fighters in the European Theater of operations. Other black pilots, navigators, bombardiers and enlisted crew personnel formed the 477th Bombardment Group (medium) flying the North American B-25. At the end of the war in Europe, elements of the two groups were joined to form the 477th Composite Group flying P-47's and B-25's. The composite group was deactivated in May 1946 and the 332nd Fighter Group was reactivated. The group continued until June 1, 1949, after President Harry S Truman integrated the Armed Forces.

Cadets

After several hours the train pulled into Cheehaw Station, Alabama. I was wearing my civilian clothes and had never before seen an army vehicle. I saw a GI truck back up to the station as I was exiting the train. Coming down the steps I heard another black soldier in uniform yell out to me, "Hit the ground, Mister!" I didn't know what he was talking about, but I caught on very quickly!

Some upperclassmen told me and other recruits to get in the truck. That was when the hazing began. I imagine it was the same thing that Benjamin O. Davis Jr. encountered when he was at West Point—the hazing and the silent treatment. B. O. Davis was already legendary in black military circles in the early 1940s. B. O. Davis Sr. had became the first black to attain the rank of general in U.S. Army history. Since his son B. O. Davis Jr. graduated from West Point his success in a military career was expected; he too achieved the rank of general.

It seems there has always been a certain amount of hazing perpetrated on military cadets. It appears that the silent treatment was a special form of hazing reserved by whites in the military for blacks with whom they might share physical space. B. O. Davis Jr. was given the silent treatment at West Point for four years. Then he was at Tuskegee six classes ahead of me, in class 42-C, the first class of black pilots to receive training. "C" stood for March, the third month and graduation date, and of course "42" was the year, 1942. I was in class 42-I. Davis's class was the first; I was a cadet in the seventh, with graduation scheduled for September. There were between fifteen and twenty young black men in each class, as I remember.

When I arrived at Tuskegee the stories about Davis Sr. and Davis Jr. were circulating. General Davis Sr. was considered a "Tom" by many blacks. (In the black world when we say "Tom" we are referring to another black person who curries favors with white persons by flattering and fawning over them.) Davis Jr. was sometimes presumed to be advancing in rank because of his father's high rank and his own degree from West Point. Evidence was offered by innuendos of ineptness in Davis Jr's. flying ability. It was alleged that at one point during his Tuskegee pilot training Davis Jr. had landed his plane on the "T." The "T" was a wooden direction indicator to show approaching pilots which way the wind was blowing so they could choose the direction in which to land; it was manually changed as needed for approaching planes. In hindsight it can be seen that these allegations about the Davises were probably sour grapes on the part of some other blacks who were jealous. At the time the history of what the Davises had endured to gain the rank they had earned was not generally known.

In situations such as theirs one has to develop a certain attitude of "I'm just as good as you are and maybe better and I'm not going to let you psychologically beat me down because my skin just happens to be darker than yours" to succeed in these games that whites have played with persons of color throughout the centuries. Some blacks seeing others of their race succeeding in spite of the hell the white world has dished out are envious. These blacks try to bring the downfall of their black peers through malicious gossip.

On the night of our arrival while on the way to the barracks, which were on the campus of Tuskegee Institute, we stopped at the warehouse and were given linens. I was very tired and just wanted to sleep at that point. The upperclassmen showed us how to make up our beds when we got to the barracks, and then they jerked the linens off all the beds. They said we were to remake them and they'd be back in five or ten minutes for inspection. When they returned, the upperclassmen had a quarter. One of them flipped the quarter in the air and when it hit the blanket it was supposed to bounce. If it didn't they would tear up the job one of us had done and we'd have to keep remaking those beds until the linens were taut enough that the quarter bounced. It was after 1:00 A.M. before the upperclassmen were finally satisfied with our bed-making abilities.

Reveille came before daybreak. We were required to "fall out" to a street near the barracks. The moon was still up, and it was so dark that the upperclassmen had to use flashlights to be able to read our names for roll call. I said to myself, "Lord have mercy! I've chosen the wrong career."

During those first weeks I wanted to cry. I hadn't known what to expect. I had to run everywhere I went. Anytime a trainee exited the stoop of his barrack and hit the ground, he had better start running. That was part of the training. The only time they did not enforce that was when we were on the flight line. They gave that part of it up then.

Mealtimes at the Tuskegee Air Base dining hall, which was on the campus of Tuskegee Institute, were unique experiences for me. There were about ten tables arranged parallel with an aisle down the middle. About eight cadets including two upperclassmen were seated at each long table. The two cadets seated on the aisle end of each table were designated as the "gunner" and the "gunner's mate," just as though they were in an aircraft. The waitress brought the food to their end of the table, handed it to the gunner, and announced the contents of the dish. The gunner would then announce to his gunner's mate, "Sir, the chicken has arrived." "Contact," the gunner's mate would reply. Then the next dish would arrive. "Sir, the macaroni has arrived," to which the gunner's mate would say, "Contact." This would continue until all food items had arrived at the table to complete that meal's menu.

In the meantime all the other cadets at the table would have to remember what dishes had been brought while sitting at attention with our eyes straight ahead. After all food items were on the table, when someone wanted to serve his plate he was required to ask in the following manner, for example: "Sir, does anyone care for chicken?" If one of the upperclassmen wanted to harass a cadet he would say, "Mister, you want it before me?" "No sir!" would be the correct reply to avoid further harassment.

Throughout the meal we were required to keep our eyes straight ahead. We could not look at the food. When we got the food on our forks we had to bring each bite to our mouths in a square motion. The smallest penalty for violating this military mealtime "etiquette" was to be required to stand at attention with your back against the nearest wall in the manner and for the length of time prescribed by the upperclassmen. The worst penalty was that you were washed out of the Army Air Corps; your rank was reduced, and you were sent to the regular army and paid twenty-one dollars a month.

When I think of the dining hall on Tuskegee's campus I always think of one of the most distinguished black Americans, Dr. George Washington Carver. Dr. Carver's laboratory was across the street from the dining hall where we ate three meals a day. Constantly I would see cars with out-of-state license plates parked outside his building. People came from all over the country to seek his counsel. I saw him almost every day when he came out of his lab. Through the window of the dining hall there was a plain view to the door of his building. Dr. Carver was exceedingly thin and quite an old man with stooped posture when I was at Tuskegee. He was also very shy. In fact, Dr. Carver was so shy that I saw him run back into his laboratory when he saw strangers come looking for him.

By that time we all knew that Dr. Carver's accomplishments as a scientist were world renowned. He was a big topic of conversation all over Tuskegee. The other cadets, like me, had come from across the country, and we were all awed by Dr. Carver's reputation. Some of the visible symbols of his work were flowers, with which he was experimenting, growing outside his lab building. One day those flowers would be one color and the next day they would be another color. He did a lot with plant research, always trying to help farmers improve their crops.

It was said that Henry Ford wanted Dr. Carver to come to work for him. One of the cadets in a class ahead of me related that one day he had been present when Dr. Carver received a letter and blank check, both signed by Ford. Ford was offering to pay Dr. Carver any amount he cared to put on the check if he would come to work for Ford in Detroit. Dr. Carver reportedly tore up the check. He was determined that by staying in Alabama and working at Tuskegee Institute he could do black people the most good. No amount of money could pull him off that purpose. I was at Tuskegee in the spring of 1942. Dr. Carver died the following January.

The cadets were an exceptional group of men from all over the country. Most of them seemed to have college degrees. They were intellectually superior as a group. Many appeared to have come from engineering backgrounds because they brought slide rules with them to Tuskegee. In classes they used them for mathematical calculations. Although I didn't own a slide rule, I had witnessed Professor Hampton D. Smith, a chemistry instructor at Claflin, make use of one when he was teaching in the science lab.

At the time we were in training we could not have imagined how famous our group of pilots would become. When Tuskegee-trained pilots got into the war zone in Europe we were assigned to fly escort for bombers. Because our airmen were believed never to have lost a bomber to enemy fire and the planes in which we flew had the tails painted red, we became known as the "Red Tailed Angels." Our story became well known in the 1980s when a full-length feature movie entitled *Tuskegee Airmen* was made. Because it is still rerun on television many Americans know something of our history.

As cadets at Tuskegee we all had one thing on our minds—becoming army pilots. There was no playing around. Each cadet's purpose was very serious in that regard. We were a determined lot and could see that in each other every day. The way a man goes about his work demonstrates his commitment to his stated outcome. Most of us had a sense of knowing that we were there to show that blacks were as capable as whites at flying aircraft. Little did we know at that time what the army's "game" was concerning us as potential black pilots. We had no idea that the white power structure was determined to prove that we as black men were not capable of becoming aircraft pilots. At the time we did not know that our situation was highly political.

The main fear I had was of being "washed out" of the program, as we termed being eliminated from pilot training, and sent to the regular army. Every cadet was fearful of that and felt intimidated. Being "washed out" not only meant personal failure but also resulted in a loss of income, putting one back into the twenty-one-dollars-per-month range.

The first five weeks at Tuskegee are mostly a blur in my mind. They were filled with learning military habits and being hazed by upperclassmen. In addition we attended classes to learn the basics of airplanes, flight theory, aviation weather, and other related fields. After five weeks we began flight training in the planes. We trained in Stearman PT-17s. These were known as "tail wheel" planes, meaning that two wheels were in front under the engine area and the third was under the tail at the rear of each aircraft.

We were provided with first-class pilot accessories and officer-training equipment such as flying jackets, helmets, and goggles. All our instructors were black. My instructor was Sherman Rose. He was an excellent teacher, as were all the instructors. The planes would hold two people, one behind the other. The instructors sat in the rear, and the cadet or student pilot sat in the front. There were dual controls, one set for the front position and one for the rear. If the student moved the stick in the front, it also moved in the back; likewise for the rudders. When we flew we had parachutes strapped to our backs. Occasionally a pilot would be forced to bail out.

Before taking off on each flight we were required to file a flight plan. When we arrived at the flight line that was the only place where we cadets were not harassed or hazed. Of course we were required to give each plane a preflight check. This consisted primarily of a visual walk around the plane as well as checking the gasoline and oil levels. Once we were inside the plane there was another list of items to be checked, but I have long forgotten those details.

Stearman PT-17s had to be hand-cranked to start the engines. That required mechanics on the ground in front of the planes and propellers. Because of the angle at which the noses of the planes were constructed, pilots could not see ahead when the planes were on the ground. As one can imagine, the mechanics were in a very dangerous position. Our communications with them had to be impeccably accurate. A mechanic's life was at risk each time we started an engine. Therefore, as pilots, we communicated orally with the mechanics before they assisted in starting the engines. Each time we were ready the same conversation would follow. The mechanic would say, "Switch off, gas on, throttle closed." A pilot would reply, "Switch off, gas on, throttle closed." Then the mechanic would say, "Contact," to which a pilot would reply, "Contact," while simultaneously turning the key in the switch of the cockpit. The mechanic would immediately pull the prop as he moved away at the same time. He had to pay close attention because, if that propeller began rotation a second before he was ready, it could kill him.

As soon as the engine caught, it would start up and smoke. We were under visual flight rules (VFR). Pilots taxied to the end of the runway in the following manner: left rudder, look, then right rudder and look; this maneuvering would result in an S pattern if viewed from above. The purpose was to be able to see where we were taxiing because the angle of the plane's nose blocked our view ahead until we were airborne.

Although our primary flight instructors were black civilians, most of our check rides were given by white pilots who were army officers. If I were being given a check ride, my name would be on the board that morning. I would go to the flight line and find the officer to whom I was assigned. As I approached him, I would stand at attention, salute, and say, "Cadet Earl Middleton reporting." Oftentimes when we saluted, the officers would not return our salutes. Seemingly this was their way of expressing their disapproval at blacks being trained to become army pilots.

I would then gather up my flying gear and head for the plane. The officer would tell me which maneuvers he wanted me to execute in the aircraft. Of course fear and intimidation were our constant companions. Anyone who has experienced military training knows that this is an ordinary component of the process. However, as blacks we were given an extra dose of insults based on our skin color.

After taxiing to the end of the runway maneuvering the aircraft in the S pattern, I would head the nose of the plane into the end of the runway at a ninety-degree angle. With my feet firmly planted on the brakes, I would shove the throttle of the plane all the way forward, revving up the engine to its full capacity for a few seconds to check the magnetos on the RPM indicator. After rechecking for any other air or ground traffic, I would ease the plane into takeoff position. Then I would make sure that the nose of the PT-17 was lined up parallel with the runway and that my rudders were equidistant from the floor so that I could ensure a straight roll down the runway. Once again I would shove the throttle all the way forward, holding it with one hand while keeping the other on the stick. The plane would move forward picking up speed every foot of the way.

One of the most intricate maneuvers in the rollout was making sure I kept the plane straight ahead through proper pressure on the rudders until I felt the plane lifting from the ground. Too much pressure on either rudder without a very quick correction would result in a ground loop. This was an extremely dangerous situation in which the plane was immediately jerked in one direction or the other heading back to the end of the runway. Or worse, the plane would leave the runway off to one side.

Once airborne and out of the vicinity of the airfield I would begin the maneuvers the senior pilot had indicated. They might consist of power-on and power-off stalls, in which there was such a loss of lift and increase in drag that the aircraft tended to drop or go out of control; spins, in which the airplane began falling rapidly with the nose down and rotating out of control; 8's on a crossroad, in which I used a straight line on the ground, such as railroad tracks, to guide me while making imaginary 8-shaped figures with the path of the plane; a chandelle, an aerial acrobatic maneuver; and lazy 8's consisting of flying-coordination training maneuvers.

All the time the white army officer would sit, saying nothing, in the rear seat with his feet on the rudders and his hand on the stick following my every move. Although he was silent, I could feel his mental criticism.

Once I had finished the prescribed maneuvers, I would head back to Moton Field and land the plane, hoping to satisfy the officer who was conducting my check ride. I would taxi the plane back to the hangar area, where we would exit the aircraft. Upon completion the white officer would say nothing. He wouldn't speak to me through the entire process.

At some point during my first few months of training, when I was dressed in my full cadet uniform, I slipped off, went up to the town of Tuskegee to a black man's photography studio, and had him take a picture of me. This photo would become very important to me in the decades ahead.

During the time I was training at Tuskegee, there was a collegiate meeting scheduled. Because most of our peers at college knew that Bernice Bryant was my girlfriend, they elected her to represent Claflin University at the meeting at Tuskegee Institute. When Bernice arrived by train, I was unable to meet her at the station because of my restrictive training schedule. I was subsequently made aware that she had arrived on the campus. She was given a room in one of the campus dormitories along with other delegates to the meeting.

While Bernice was at Tuskegee, we had only a brief time together. I told her I was going to check out a plane and do some flying so she could witness my progress. I did a flying demonstration for her of what I had learned in my pilot training. Of course, she remained on the ground. Bernice was quite proud of me when she saw how I could pilot the plane, perform the maneuvers, and land the plane safely. It was wonderful to have the opportunity to show Bernice around at Tuskegee. This was probably sometime in March or April of 1942. Our time together there was so short we did not even have an opportunity to discuss my flight.

Because I had joined the Army Air Corps in February, my final semester of academic work at Claflin University had been interrupted. To ensure that I would graduate with my class I studied my college courses at night after I was at Tuskegee. This was on my own time so as not to interfere with pilot training. Several other cadets in the barracks seemed to be doing likewise. Bernice kept me abreast of the school assignments. She mailed the schedule for the class work, and I would do the assignments and send them back. Also she made sure I was fulfilling the administrative requirements for receiving my degree. Her mother, Gertrude Dangerfield Bryant, was employed in the university president's office and helped too. With their assistance I was able to complete my course requirements and march with my class for graduation.

Washed

Very shortly following Bernice's visit to Tuskegee my name appeared on the board at the airfield for a check ride. I didn't know why. After the check ride I was told I had been washed out of the training program. No reason was given. My flight instructor, Sherman Rose, was shocked, as was "Chief" Charles A. Anderson, director of pilot training at Tuskegee. They both declared that my performance had been up to standards in every respect.

Being eliminated from the pilot training program was the biggest disappointment of my young life. Knowing who I am helped me get through it, and I was able to give a positive report about the program to a fellow Claflinite and boyhood friend, Curtis C. Robinson, when he approached me at graduation to inquire about the Army Air Corps pilot training at Tuskegee. I encouraged him and filled him in on some of the expectations and pitfalls to look for if he decided on it. Curtis did become a Tuskegee Airman; he graduated in Class 43-D, was commissioned, and flew missions during World War II. He served with great distinction, as did almost every single man trained at Tuskegee. After the war Curtis became a pharmacist, and to the best of my knowledge he still works at that profession in Washington, D.C. After he published his memoirs several years ago, I had the pleasure of joining him for a celebration at Claflin. Our families remain friends to this day.

At that time we did not understand that "the powers that be" in the system were determined to prove that blacks were unable to pilot planes. It's a miracle that the pilot training program at Tuskegee was even initiated. According to *The Tuskegee Airmen,* by Lynn M. Homan and Thomas Reilly, several studies were made after World War I regarding the role of African Americans in the military. It seems the studies were designed to prove blacks were inferior to whites and could perform only in menial positions. A January 1941 lawsuit by a black Howard University student, Yancey Williams, over rejection of his application as a flying cadet was evidently the impetus for the War Department's announcement that same month that African Americans would be allowed to become Air Corps pilots. In *The Tuskegee Airmen—Black Heroes of World War II* Jacqueline Harris tells us that black leaders Walter White, A. Philip Randolph, and T. Arnold Hill met in 1940 with President Franklin D. Roosevelt to discuss the use of blacks in the armed services. Years earlier the *Pittsburgh Courier* had launched a campaign to open all branches of the service to blacks.

A large measure of credit is owed to Eleanor Roosevelt, the wife of FDR, for the program's initiation. According to Lt. Col. (retired) Charles W. Dryden in his book *A-Train: Memoirs of a Tuskegee Airman,* Mrs. Roosevelt went to Tuskegee Institute in 1940 seeking information on a polio-treatment facility at the hospital on behalf of her husband. While there she learned that airplanes she saw flying around the area were piloted by Negroes. Her curiosity led to an introduction to Chief Anderson. At her request, Chief Anderson took her for a ride. She then *knew* that blacks were every bit as competent as whites at piloting an airplane. On her return to Washington she urged the president to remove the barriers to Negroes in the Army Air Corps. Tuskegee Institute was chosen as the site for pilot training because there was already a civilian pilot training program for blacks under way there. Still there was much official doubt in the system about blacks' ability to pilot an aircraft. This fact was exhibited every day in every way to us as black pilots in training.

Evidently it had been decided that there would be a quota on how many blacks would be graduated as pilots. The quota had nothing to do with qualifications or flying ability. As far as I know, no official explanation has ever been given as to how those to be washed out were selected. According to Alan M. Osur in his book *Blacks in the Army Air Forces during World War II: The Problem of Race Relations,* published by the Office of Air Force History in 1977, "The AAF plan provided for the training of only 45 black officers during the first year of operation." Of course, I entered pilot training during that first year of operation, and there were over a dozen cadets who started. With a new class coming in monthly, in a year's time that would have amounted to a total of several hundred cadets, at least, beginning training. Graduation carried with it a rank of second lieutenant, the lowest rank of officer. With a quota that we now know was only forty-five officers per year, that automatically meant that the wash-out rate had to be more than half of those entering pilot training. That part of the question has been answered. However, the mystery of how the washed-out cadets were chosen remains. There appears to have been no systematic process, the whim of the white officers was the deciding factor.

Gilbert Cargill, one of the civilian instructors in the early 1940s, had this to say many years later:

> I cannot document this, but we instructors felt that in many cases men were washed out or eliminated because of some quota system set up determining the number of black pilots. . . . I lost some cadets, washed out, who were natural pilots; they were good. These washouts were picked at random by the air force people without consulting the instructors. The white officers who did the picking were not working with the cadets so they had no way of judging their ability.
>
> Whenever a cadet went for an unannounced check ride he was through. If he happened to be a student of mine who I might think was the greatest and he was tagged for a check ride I could write him off. They had a hearing afterwards but it was just a matter of form. It was unfortunate, for some of those fellows were very disappointed. They knew they had a natural talent for flying; you know when something's right for you. Cadets could be eliminated in this manner right through the three phases of training. I would be willing to bet that 70 to 80 percent of those eliminated by this means should have passed.

Although my sense of self-worth helped me cope with being washed from the program, because I didn't know about the quota system, I couldn't help but feel for many years afterward that I had failed at one of the most important things in my life. For years I never mentioned the fact that I had been at Tuskegee to anyone who hadn't known already. Because I had been washed and did not graduate from flight training and get my wings, I did not feel that I was a Tuskegee Airman. Only in recent years have I come to realize that being washed out was not indicative of my lack of ability as a pilot. It is now known that there were very few men who got to Tuskegee who could not pass muster as a pilot.

When I was washed from the program I was stripped of all the training pins I had been awarded and was required to turn in my pilot accessories, logbook, and all uniform items I had been issued. I was then shipped to Maxwell Field, another army base about fifty miles north of Tuskegee near Montgomery, Alabama. Bernice was shocked when she received a letter from me saying that I had been washed and was now stationed at Maxwell.

The other black soldiers at Maxwell knew who had been shipped in from Tuskegee. They scorned those of us who had come from there as they considered us elitist. There was a different caliber of men at Maxwell than I had left at Tuskegee. Whereas the pilot cadets had been serious about their endeavors, at Maxwell the flagrant use of profanity, gambling, and other less than desirable pursuits were engaged in by a majority of the men. This type of behavior was a shock to me at that time; being from a strict Methodist background, I was flabbergasted. However, there were some men at Maxwell who had higher aspirations, and that was encouraging.

At Maxwell Field I was assigned to the all-black Fourth Aviation Squadron, commanded by a white man, Capt. Morton B. Howell. We had dress parades on a regular basis. One day following a parade, in front of the entire squadron, Captain Howell said, "Middleton, I want to see you in my office!" "Yes sir," I replied. When we got inside he said, "At ease," and that made me feel better. He went on to say that he had a situation he wanted me to handle. He made me the mail clerk and put me in charge of the squadron post office. Although I didn't know it at the time, Captain Howell had graduated from Yale Law School just a few months before. He had served a brief stint at Scott Field in St. Louis before assuming command of the Fourth Aviation Squadron at Maxwell Field in Montgomery. Along with this new responsibility of being squadron postmaster came a promotion from private to staff sergeant. Of course this meant a salary increase, but that still did not put my pay back up anywhere close to what I had been making as a cadet at Tuskegee.

Certain privileges came along with being staff sergeant. One of these perks was that I had a private room in the barrack. My brother Sam was assigned to the army post at Ft. Gordon, Georgia, where he taught academic subjects to other soldiers. Sam was shocked when he came to visit and found I had a private room. He could stay there in the same room with me while he was visiting. The barracks housing black soldiers were about a mile away from those housing the white soldiers. We were way down at the end of the runway near where the planes took off.

When I was stationed at Maxwell Field there were white officers and black enlisted men. That was about the extent of army integration at the time. In recent years Morton Howell reminded me of the names of some of the commanding officers of our Fourth Aviation Squadron. Some of them were Major Wilhelm; Capt. Chester D. Shepherd of Massachusetts, near Boston; Capt. Morgan Odman of Hartford, Connecticut; Capt. Lansing B. Mays of Albany, Georgia; and Capt. Robert Shelor from upstate South Carolina. Howell also reminded me that the names of some of the other enlisted men in the unit with which I served were Sergeant Russell, Cpl. Warren Moment, (Mess) Sergeant Paige, S.SGT. Grover Chiles, Cpl. Roosevelt Appling, S.SGT. Johnny Richards, Corporal Johnson, and Staff Sergeant Jackson.

The Quartermaster Platoons, the 942nd and the 943rd, also had quarters in our area and were commanded by Lieutenants Stewart and Rothchild. One of them had a first sergeant named Hanger, a big, tall, heavy man. Lieutenant Rothchild was in charge of the motor pool and later was promoted to captain.

Three men with the same surname were 1st Sgt. Roy Johnson, an old Twenty-fourth Infantry master sergeant retreaded for World War II; Sgt. Earnest Johnson of the Quartermaster; and Sgt. Murphy Johnson, who was basically a carpenter but was assigned to duty as drill sergeant and in maintenance. There was another orderly room sergeant named Walton, and Sgt. Hazzard Parks from Virginia was the chief clerk. Sergeant Edwards, a mess sergeant, possessed great skill and legendary talent in the culinary line. I can still taste his hash brown potatoes now sixty years later!

The Boxers

During World War II the military sponsored entertainment for soldiers. Joe Louis and Sugar Ray Robinson served in the U.S. Armed Forces for the purpose of giving exhibition fights to entertain the troops. When the boxers came to Maxwell Field, they were assigned to stay in my room with me, so we were roommates while they were on the base. I had a large private room that served as an appropriate accommodation for these VIP sports figures, who were already well known by this time as champions in the ring. Louis, the older of the two, was the heavyweight champion of the world at this time.

Louis and Robinson were both in prime physical shape. As members of the military they were dressed in uniform when out of the boxing ring. When they arrived at my room I told them everyone was excited that they were going to fight at our base. Then I briefly explained the segregation policy on base, and they expressed concern. At that time segregation by race was the rule, *and* this was Montgomery, Alabama. By the time Louis and Robinson arrived at Maxwell Field the word had gotten out that black soldiers would be assigned seats in the rear and only whites would be at ringside for the fight. Black soldiers were mad as hell about that.

Shortly after the boxers arrived a group of blacks from my squadron came to my room to meet with them and let them know we could get no ringside seats even though the boxers themselves were black. Louis and Robinson were incensed about this and raised the devil with the base commanders. Eventually the higher-ups relented and let a few black soldiers sit ringside. During their exhibition fight Louis and Robinson spit on the floor and in other ways showed their disapproval of the way blacks were being treated.

Kilby Prison

In connection with entertainment and recreation, the army brass was always looking for suitable activities for the troops. We were definitely underutilized manpower. Our assignments were decided by the white commanders above Captain Howell, and they seemed to have a dilemma about what to do with black soldiers. Anything of a nondestructive nature to keep us occupied was attractive to them. The race thing had them baffled.

One of the activities they settled on was baseball. We had teams on the base and were matched up for games. At some point in 1943 it was decided by the higher-ups that we would go over to Kilby Prison, located in Montgomery, and play against the teams there, where we were pitted against all-black teams made up of prisoners. In the minds of the white commanders, evidently, a black man was a black man regardless of whether he was defending his country from foreign aggressors or serving time for alleged or committed crimes.

At this time some of the Scottsboro Boys were still imprisoned at Kilby. In 1931 nine young blacks had been falsely accused of raping two white women on a freight train traveling from Chattanooga, Tennessee, into Alabama. The case had come before an all-white jury in Scottsboro, Alabama, and become a cause célèbre because of the lack of evidence and the speed with which the men were convicted. Three times their convictions by the Alabama juries were appealed to the U.S. Supreme Court, and three times they were overturned, but Alabama juries kept reconvicting them. Five of the youths were finally freed after languishing for about seven years in prison. However, in the early 1940s while I was there playing ball, several of the Scottsboro Boys were still at Kilby. Whether or not any of them were playing ball, I can't say. Going into a prison situation, which was a new experience for me, a person just didn't ask that type of question. By 1950 the last of the Scottsboro Boys had been freed from prison— whether by parole, appeal, or escape.

Montgomery Buses and Brutality

There were separate USOs for blacks and whites in Montgomery The USO (United Services Organization) provided wholesome recreation for the military troops during our leave time. They had locations near military bases. Food was served, and usually there were pool tables and card games available. Young ladies from the area were invited to come in and meet soldiers there. No gambling was allowed, and there were plenty of chaperones on hand to ensure proper behavior between the sexes. If a soldier met a girl at the USO and she liked him, her family might invite him to their home for dinner.

Shortly after being shipped to Maxwell, I met Miss Johnnie Mae Love at the Montgomery USO. She had very light skin, almost white, and was well dressed. She had a friendly nature and a beautiful attitude, and we immediately hit it off. Johnnie Mae had a very nice family who lived in downtown Montgomery and constantly made me welcome in their home. We dated for most of the time I was at Maxwell. When the subject of marriage came up, I told her that in the event of my war-time death I wanted to make sure my mother was the beneficiary of my ten-thousand-dollar government insurance policy. At the same time I omitted telling her of the feelings I still had for Bernice. Sometime after I left Montgomery I learned with regret that Johnnie Mae had died.

When members of my squadron and I left the base and went into the city of Montgomery we were required to ride in the back of the bus (Jim Crow laws again). We got on in the front and put our dimes in the coin box; then we were required to GET BACK OFF THE BUS AND GO TO THE BACK DOOR TO GET BACK ON AGAIN! Many times the driver would close the door and begin to pull off before we could get to the back door. Soldiers had to be back on base by 11:00 P.M. Oftentimes when these white bus drivers slammed the doors in black soldiers' faces, it would really cause the soldiers problems because it would make them late getting back and they would be disciplined for that. It was hell!

One of the days when I was on leave and went into downtown Montgomery, a gentleman approached me. He was white, Caucasian. At that time a white person wouldn't ordinarily consider speaking to a black on the streets, so for him to initiate a conversation was unusual in itself. He asked me how I enjoyed being in the army. I told him I didn't think very much of it. I explained to him about the violence that was being perpetrated in areas of Montgomery where black soldiers were on leave visiting their girlfriends, going to movies, and otherwise enjoying their well-earned time off base. "I want you to do something for me. I want you to write these reports up that you're telling me about," he requested. I replied, "I don't know who you are. How am I going to get them to you?" He said, "Drop them in a mailbox."

I don't know what caused him to come to me. This man's seeming sincerity and concern about the harassment of black soldiers convinced me to write the reports and send them. I wrote letters about the treatment blacks were receiving and how white civilians treated black soldiers off base. Over several years when I was in Montgomery, I put these reports in envelopes and dropped them in mailboxes. I didn't keep any copies. The man didn't tell me his name, but he must have given me an address. After all these years I don't remember it, and whether he received them or not, I don't know. It's been a mystery in my life. It could be that he was a member of a federal or military investigative agency.

The harsh treatment of black servicemen on the streets in Montgomery was another reason I agreed to write the reports. I know of black men who were shot, stabbed, got their throats cut, or were otherwise killed. It was terrible, terrible. These crimes were being committed by some police who were rioting in concert with military police (MPs).

During World War II the MPs would ride with the city police in Montgomery, and together they would hound the black servicemen. I imagine they treated black civilians that way too, but I was not associated with black civilians. They struck and beat a lot of black servicemen. Once after I came into Montgomery on the train, I got off at the station and walked up to the main street. Just about the time I got to the corner where the drugstore was, I made a right turn, looked down the street, and saw a white shoot a black fella, a serviceman, and kill him. All kinds of talk was going on about what happened when I got back to my barrack at Maxwell Field.

Many stories were told of how black soldiers were brutally treated on the buses and in the streets of Montgomery. We reported these to our captain, Chester D. Shepherd, from Boston. He expressed concern and mentioned on several occasions that he was planning to do something about the situation. However, we could not then see what could be accomplished because such behavior was so entrenched in Montgomery, Alabama. Some white soldiers from northern states who were serving in Montgomery were considered Yankees by Alabamians. These northerners were often treated like blacks. We saw it regularly in the heart of the city's downtown.

Once I saw a black woman get on a bus before a white group of people, and a white soldier, who I assumed was a southerner, snatched her off and said he was getting on before her. The biggest fight I saw in that town was between the northerners and the southerners over the black woman's boarding the bus on before the white man. It nearly turned into a riot. I'm talking about a hellhole they called Montgomery! I had seen nothing like that in South Carolina. It is not surprising that an incident on an Alabama bus is what sparked the civil rights movement of the 1950s and 1960s. The situation had been building up for years.

During the three years I spent at Maxwell Field, the manpower of the black soldiers was basically wasted. The main job of the blacks was to roll coal in wheelbarrows to the barracks where the white soldiers resided. In addition they planted and tended a so-called victory garden. I say "they" because my duties as postmaster consumed my day.

In the evenings and on weekends I cut other soldiers' hair in my room to make extra income. By this method I was able to bring my earnings back up to the amount I had been receiving when I was a cadet at Tuskegee. One technique I used to increase business was to do the haircuts and extend credit to soldiers. When they received their pay each month I was there with the money to cash their paychecks and collect what they owed me for the haircuts. I kept the records in an account book and had to keep the cash on hand to accomplish this.

As I accumulated money, I would send it home to Mama for safekeeping. The amounts would range from fifty to two hundred dollars. She deposited that money in an account at the bank in Orangeburg in my name. In this manner I began to build a reserve for future use and to discipline myself to save money. In the early 1940s the thought of calling home to ask Daddy for money was "off the radar screen"; it never would have entered my head.

General Tom

One morning at Maxwell Field the whistle blew about 4:30 or 5:00 in the morning. We were told to "fall out." That was the term they used to get us outside and into formation. When we were assembled, Gen. B. O. Davis Sr. made his appearance. We, as black soldiers, had made constant complaints about army segregation. Some soldiers had written him about the treatment blacks were receiving in our area of Maxwell Field quite a distance from where the white soldiers were housed. Some of these complaints concerned our doing useless and demeaning work. For example, as part of the so-called victory garden black soldiers were required to till the soil as "human mules." Yes, I mean that a plow would be attached to a few soldiers by straps, and they were required to pull those plows through the ground as though they were animals. Of course all the planting was done by hand, as were all the other garden chores.

General Davis Sr. was sent by his high command to meet with us about the situation. They had obviously given him orders about what to convey. He, in effect, said that taking all these racial insults was part of our job.

General Davis Sr. was the officer designated to do the "dirty work" of helping the higher-ups in the system perpetuate segregation. In essence he conveyed to us that we were to keep our mouths shut and take it! This explained the reputation he developed among black soldiers of being a "Tom" and why he was resented for carrying out the white men's orders in regard to blacks. In defense of General Davis Sr., all I can say is that he was between the proverbial rock and a hard place.

The way the general handled his job was in contrast to the way another, well-known black American of that era, William H. Hastie, worked. In 1943 Hastie resigned his high government position as civilian aide to the secretary of war over the military's discrimination against black officers and soldiers. His resignation made it impossible for the War Department to continue to evade the consequences of its long-practiced Jim Crow policies.

Witness to Surrender

In April 1945, after nearly three years at Maxwell Field, Alabama, I received orders to be shipped out overseas with the 129th Port Battalion.

There has always been a question in my mind about why I and so many other soldiers were kept at Maxwell Field for almost three years while the war was raging in Europe and the Pacific. Doubts about the abilities of blacks to perform on the battlefield were widespread among many in authority. Whether that had any bearing on it, I don't know, but we now know that we were probably being readied for an invasion of the Japanese mainland.

The other soldiers and I who were transferred to the 129th Port Battalion were routed through a base at Newport News, Virginia. There we loaded ships for a period of time. The ships had Plimsoll marks on the sides. We loaded each ship until the appropriate Plimsoll mark was at water level. The particular mark was chosen according to which body of water the ship would sail on. Even though I had a college degree, the army assigned me to performing heavy labor. The army commanders cared nothing about the fact that with a college degree I might be performing more valuable services. Because my skin was black they were apparently interested only in my strong back.

Throughout the World War II period, in an effort to recruit men to volunteer for military service, posters and ads depicted a bearded white man in a top hat proclaiming "Uncle Sam wants you!" The picture of the white man symbolized to me that black soldiers were taken for granted. It definitely conveyed to me and other black soldiers that the white man was in charge and that we had no significant input in his decisions.

From Newport News we were shipped to Seattle, Washington, our port of embarkation for the Pacific. En route we received news on April 12, 1945, that President Franklin D. Roosevelt had died. I will always remember where I was when I heard the news, for President Roosevelt was a giant among men during that era as head of the strongest power in the Allied nations. His presence was felt throughout the world, and his death was a landmark in most adult lives, including mine.

President Roosevelt's passing overshadowed everything else in our minds as we whiled away the next several days in Seattle waiting to ship out. By April 17 we were on the troop carrier *Kota Inten* heading toward Hawaii, Okinawa, and Ie Shima in the far Pacific.

Once we were aboard, the days and nights turned into weeks. The main pastime for the troops was gambling. Prior to this time I'd been at Maxwell Field and the Newport News shipyard (and away from my Methodist roots) for about three years. Aboard the carrier ship I began gambling out of boredom. I had learned to shoot craps at Maxwell.

We played in the latrine. Inside the door there was an entry or waiting area for when it was crowded. Around the corner were stalls housing about eight or ten commodes and probably a like number with urinals. The area also held washbasins. With perhaps more than a thousand men aboard, there were several latrines throughout the gigantic ship. The first man to get to one and spread his blanket was in control of a game. There was room for only one or maybe two blankets in each latrine. Since there was no racial segregation on the troop carrier the crap games were also integrated.

In each game there would be about eight players plus side betters. In games where I found luck with me, I had a prearrangement with a buddy that allowed me to increase my winnings. John Gregg was a fraternity brother from Orangeburg who happened also to be on the huge carrier. John and I had both pledged Phi Beta Sigma at Claflin University, and we had played football together there too.

As my money piled up I knew that, if I were perceived by the others as winning too much of their money, they would try to take it from me while I slept. This was where John's help came in. After I had accumulated a certain amount, John would come by and demand, "Give me the money you owe me!" I would give him a hunk, which he would secure. Or he would come by and ask to borrow money from me. Either way he would get the money off my person for safekeeping. In addition, if I started losing too much, John would not let me gamble it all away. He would give me back only so much with which to continue playing. John acted as my safety deposit box.

During this multiweek trip aboard the troop carrier in the Pacific, my total winnings came to about seventeen thousand dollars. Reflecting on this, I think the winnings probably came to me for two reasons: luck and the nerve to put big money in the game. During much of the remainder of this journey, I slept with the fabulous sum in a money belt around my waist. I had to be cautious because others might cut the belt from my waist while I was sleeping. John too kept the money in his waist pouch.

When I arrived at Ie Shima I sent the money to Bernice in Atlanta. By this time we were engaged to be married, and she was in graduate school at Atlanta University. There is no way I could have sent it to Mama because she knew I couldn't have earned that much. And questions about things like that are not what a soldier wants to hear from his mother.

The trip across the Pacific took more than a month. The captain of the *Kota Inten* was obliged to take an irregular course to evade submarines and enemy fire. This probably added two weeks to the cruise. My assignment in the Pacific was on the island of Ie Shima, about three miles west of the northern part of Okinawa. A small island in the Ryukyu chain, it is about five miles wide and about four hundred miles southeast of Japan. We reached Ie Shima on July 5.

As the *Kota Inten* cruised into the shore area of Ie Shima for our disembarkation, Japanese kamikaze pilots were at work, and one came very close to blowing up our ship. With great effort our gunner was able to blast the enemy plane at the last possible second. In fact debris from the exploding aircraft fell on our vessel, and many men had to jump overboard into the shallow ocean near shore to avoid being killed or maimed. Even so, several were killed. The gunner, handling a huge weapon, was strapped into position for maximum leverage in firing from his station. As soon as he saw that he had gunned down the would-be bomber and was successful at saving the carrier loaded with troops, he collapsed with mental and physical exhaustion.

Despite this "welcome" at Ie Shima, most of the main battles there had occurred while we were en route on the troop carrier. When we arrived, we learned that the well-known war correspondent Ernie Pyle had been killed during the fighting there on April 18. It seems that he was on his way to the front lines with a commander when a machine gun hidden in the coral slopes alongside their route sent them to a ditch for cover. Civilian Pyle made the same mistake that has gotten so many soldiers killed in wars—he raised his head too quickly and at the wrong time. He was hit below the rim of his helmet and killed instantly. Before I was shipped home in 1946, I saw the marker that was placed over Pyle's grave. Many of the soldiers, including me, made photos of his grave.

During the time I was stationed on Ie Shima, we not only encountered sniper fire from a small remainder of resistance on the island, but we also had regular air-raid visits from Japanese planes. Usually the air raids were at night, but sometimes they came during daylight hours. It was definitely a combat situation.

I remember digging foxholes and staying in them for the night. I had a special way of constructing my foxhole so that I could stand in it with my rifle at the ready and see in any direction. The enemy snipers would crawl on the ground on their bellies with their rifles in their hands or laid across their arms at the elbows if they wanted to use their knees to crawl faster. If a soldier was down in his foxhole he could not see them coming until they were literally on top of him and stabbing him with their bayonets. To avoid this situation I dug my hole deeper to be able to stand. I then installed four pylons made from the trunks of native bamboo or palm trees at the corners. Over the pylons I constructed a wooden cover and camouflaged it with limbs and brush from the trees. Of course I was standing in water; the water table on the island was very high, only a few feet down from the surface. Nonetheless I was able to protect myself in this manner. I learned to sleep standing up. A wet hole was my home for the seven and a half months I spent on Ie Shima. As I remember, it was monsoon season, and that added to the wet misery. I was never completely dry during the time I spent on that island.

Some nights the whole island would shake from the American artillery guns being fired to protect it. The enemy had constructed an elaborate system of tunnels in the hills of Ie Shima from which they were still resisting.

We had to be extremely alert to survive. The price for doing otherwise could be one's life. One day several other soldiers and I were policing the island. As we walked along, the man next to me was talking about leaving on the next rotation. His mind was on going home. As his brain was thus engaged, his eyes saw an object protruding from the earth in front of his next step. Without thinking about it he bent over to retrieve the wire. It was attached to a booby trap. Unfortunately, his body was the perfect target; it caught him in his chest right at the heart. The medical unit was behind us to deal with wounded soldiers and casualties. We had to keep moving. However, we could see immediately that they placed his body in a mattress cover, which served as a body bag for removal to the morgue. Death was just an instant away each day that we were on Ie Shima.

Usually strategic overall battle plans are not made known to soldiers in the field. Still the rumors fly. We heard that we were on Ie Shima to become part of an invasion of the Japanese mainland. I was afraid that, if American forces invaded Japan, a lot of our soldiers would lose their lives because of the foreign terrain. I knew that I could be one of them and that it would be a terrible slaughter of Allied forces. We were fortunate that "the man from Missouri" came up with another plan.

One day while we were on Ie Shima, we were issued gas masks, but we were never given the command to use them. We found out a couple of days later that atomic bombs had been dropped on the Japanese cities of Hiroshima and Nagasaki. Harry S Truman, who had become president when Franklin D. Roosevelt died, had decided that the best way to put a stop to the war was by using this weapon of ultimate destruction.

We were about five hundred miles from ground zero on the days the atomic bombs were dropped, but of course we were unaware of what was transpiring at the time. Although I realize fully the havoc the bombs and resulting radiation wreaked on the lives of the innocent Japanese people, I am still grateful for, and in support of, the decision President Truman made to use them. Saying this may sound selfish, but there is much more involved. President Truman was justified in doing whatever it took to put a halt to the war. Although the bombing cost the lives of thousands of innocent people, it saved the lives of millions of others.

After the atomic bombs were dropped on Hiroshima and Nagasaki, Japanese emperor Hirohito decided to surrender. President Truman accepted the offer and appointed Gen. Douglas MacArthur to plan and conduct the official signing of the surrender. He notified the Japanese that he wanted a meeting with a delegation of sixteen Japanese officials in the Philippines. Word came that their deputation, headed by Lt. Gen. Torashiro Kawabe, the Japanese army's deputy chief of staff, would be flying in to Ie Shima on August 17, 1945, on their way to Manila for the intermediate surrender meeting.

Because the Japanese had operated with such trickery up to this point, our Allied commanders on Ie Shima were very cautious about letting Japanese planes land on the island. Our commanders sent word that the planes had to be painted white with green crosses on the sides of the fuselages and on the top and bottom of each wing when they came in or they would be shot out of the sky. Additionally the planes had to be capable of in-flight voice communications in English on a specific frequency. The exact date and hour the planes would depart from Sata Misaki on the southern tip of Kyushu, the route and altitude of their flight, and the estimated time of arrival in Ie Shima would be broadcast six hours in advance in English from Tokyo on a stated frequency. Their headquarters had to acknowledge receipt of the broadcast prior to takeoff. The planes were required to approach Ie Shima on a course of 180 degrees and circle the landing field at one thousand feet or below the cloud layer until joined by an escort of U.S. Army P-38s, which would lead them to a landing. They were further informed that the escort might join the planes prior to their arrival at Ie Shima.

When the two Mitsubishi bombers—nicknamed "Betty Bombers" by American troops—landed at the Ie Shima airfield, I was fortunate to get photos of this small piece of history. The Japanese officials were transferred to C-54s and flown on to Manila, where a preliminary surrender document was signed. About two weeks later, on September 2, when leaders of all the Allied powers could come to Japan to represent their nations, the official surrender ceremony was conducted aboard the battleship *Missouri* anchored in Tokyo Bay.

Of course, as a foot soldier on the ground at the time the events were transpiring, I had no idea, until years later, how all these pieces of the scenario fit together. For example, when we got the story about the Japanese planes landing at Ie Shima, it was said that the officials were "coming to surrender." That story, as a piece of the overall picture, was true as far as it went, but there were many other parts to the big picture of how the surrender was carried out. At that time probably President Truman and only a handful of his top commanders, advisers, and allies had knowledge of the entire plan to end the war. It has been enlightening to me personally to look back and contemplate the role I played and the locations in which I found myself in relation to events in history.

During the war years I was in the right places at the right times to avoid horrendous battles and certain death. It appears that troops of which I was a part were intended for an invasion of Japan. Fortunately for me personally and for all Americans and our allies, President Truman had a better plan for ending the war.

After the official surrender we were not immediately shipped back to the United States. There were thousands of troops in faraway countries, and it took months to secure troop carriers for the trip home. On January 8, 1946, I was finally shipped back to the United States. My ship arrived in California on January 20. The voyage home was quicker than the one to the Pacific theater because in peacetime evasive cruising was unnecessary and we could follow a set course.

On January 28, 1946, I was mustered out of the army at Ft. Gordon, Georgia. When I looked at my discharge papers I saw that the time I had served at Tuskegee had not been recorded. I immediately called this to the attention of those in charge, but THEY REFUSED TO INCLUDE THE RECORD OF MY SERVICE AT TUSKEGEE TRAINING TO BECOME A PILOT. As far as I can ascertain, this information still does not appear on any official army records. Research conducted at the National Archives revealed that my name does not appear with the group in the class of 42-I. Only the actual graduates and a couple of cadets who washed a short time before graduation are named in these records. They appeared to have been culled from a larger number of related items. I understand that many of the individual records of World War II servicemen were destroyed in a 1970s St. Louis fire.

Fortunately I have documentation of my training at Tuskegee in the form of the photograph made in my cadet uniform. That I slipped off and went uptown to have it made one day during my training months was, in hindsight, a very smart move on my part. Recently I learned that the man who made this photo was a famous photographer, P. H. Polk. My Army Separation Qualification Record does state that I had "A.A.F. Basic Tng.," and of course, the only place the U.S. Army Air Force was training black men was Tuskegee.

4

Orangeburg

A Partner for Life

During my military years I became very adept as a barber. Over the three years I was stationed at Maxwell Field, I averaged about twenty haircuts a week in my spare time. When I returned home to Orangeburg in 1946, barbering was my easiest route to earning a living. I knew I didn't want to teach, and I didn't want to preach. My preparation and talents were not suitable for these two professions, which some other members of my family had traditionally pursued very successfully. Within walking distance of our home was a barbershop where I could begin earning money immediately. This shop was owned by William Davis and was located on the so-called Railroad Corner across from South Carolina State and Claflin.

With the war ended, some savings accumulated, and a steady income, I was now in a position to consider proposing marriage to Bernice. Although we had grown up in the same neighborhood, our romance had really begun to blossom during our freshman year together at Claflin University. By the time I left to go into pilot training at Tuskegee in February 1942, we were "going together."

During most of the years I served in World War II, Bernice attended graduate school at Atlanta University. While I was stationed at Maxwell Air Force Base, I visited her there when I could. I had purchased an engagement ring for Bernice when I was stationed at Montgomery, but I did not want to tie her to a commitment before the war was ended. In my mind the worst case scenario would not have been my death but rather a disabling injury. I did not want her to be obligated to me while that was a possibility.

Fortunately for me, as soon as the war ended, Bernice was ready to accept my proposal. We were married on February 10, 1946, at our home church in Orangeburg, Trinity Methodist. Bernice was twenty-three years old, and I was twenty-six. Our pastor, the Reverend I. DeQuincey New-man, performed the ceremony. On a Sunday at the conclusion of the morning worship service Bernice and I exchanged our marriage vows. Bernice was radiantly beautiful in her wedding dress. With the congregation of families and friends present the church was full.

During my years in the military I had made a close friendship with a white army captain, Chester D. Shepherd, from near Boston, Massachusetts. He had discussed more than once with me the possibility of my moving to that area at war's end. After Bernice and I married we seriously considered moving. We knew there were more possibilities for black professionals to advance in the North than in the South, and we kept our minds open on the subject. There is no question that we could have earned more money and attained more prestigious positions if we'd moved from the South. Besides the more tolerant racial attitudes that apparently prevailed in the Northeast and the West in the postwar 1940s, those areas were much more populated and offered more opportunities because of the greater population density.

Two of my brothers, James and Phillip, moved to California right after the war. Both married their South Carolina sweethearts. James married Inez Williams of Elloree, South Carolina. They lived in California all their married lives and raised their children there. After James passed in 1990, Inez continued to make her home in Los Angeles. She and their daughter, Harriett, still live there. Phillip married Vivian Scott of Norway, South Carolina, in a California ceremony after the war. They lived in Los Angeles and Colorado until about ten years ago, when they moved to Atlanta. Both James and Phillip were builders all their working lives after they finished their military service.

My sister Dorothy Louise taught school in Rock Hill, South Carolina, until she retired back home to Orangeburg. Helen, our oldest sister, taught in Orangeburg. Our oldest brother, Sam, married the former Verona Wakefield. They both taught in Orangeburg, and Sam was a principal and school administrator before his retirement.

Bernice's brother, Butch (Alonzo W. Bryant Jr.), has lived in southern California all his adult life and still resides there. He was an architect before his retirement.

Bernice and I really wanted to stay in the South. We saw some positives in remaining near our roots and being in a small town. Mainly we believed that we would be better positioned to raise the children we hoped to have in a small-town environment. We knew that to be near extended family members with the values and Christian principles we wanted to instill, staying in Orangeburg would be best. Although Jim Crow laws were still in effect and segregation of the races was as firmly entrenched as ever, we still lived in "another world" in Orangeburg. Our world, the one Bernice and I had grown up in, was self-contained. We had our church, our families, our friends, our work, "our" stores, and "our" side of town. By that point in time too, southern whites knew that, if they were going to keep blacks out of "their" public schools, they had to at least make a pretense of providing equal facilities for blacks.

Our families had no enemies or personal animosities in Orangeburg's white community, and in some cases we had some personal friendships there. There was another huge asset in Orangeburg. That was the presence of two historically black schools of higher education, Claflin and South Carolina State.

By this time Bernice was teaching library science at South Carolina State College. After our marriage we roomed at her parents' home on Dunton Street for a few months and then rented a house nearby on Goff Avenue. The house is still there today. It was a five-room frame house with running water for the kitchen sink but no indoor bath facilities. We called that setup "five rooms and a path." (A bath has since been added.) I remember the rent was ten dollars per month. This is where we lived when our first child, Anita Louise, was born in 1947.

At that time Papa was in some of his final years before retirement as a teacher in the carpentry shop at South Carolina State. On his way home each day after work his walking route took him by our rented home. After Anita started walking and would see him coming, she would run out and hug him. Because we lived in close proximity to my parents and Papa would pass by daily during our early married years, he and Anita developed a special bond during her young years and his later ones. Already our decision to remain in Orangeburg was paying off in terms of life's intangible but irreplaceable assets.

Papa Goes Home

In 1952, several years after he retired from teaching, Papa took sick. He developed kidney disease. I remember taking him in my car to the hospital the last time. It was February and cold in Orangeburg. Mama wrapped him up well with warm socks, overcoat, and hat. Dr. Monroe Crawford

Sr. was Papa's regular physician, but since this trip was an emergency he was treated by Dr. Hyman Marcus. Papa's heart was giving out, evidently from the effects of kidney problems. The sophisticated medical devices in use today for treating patients were unheard of in the early 1950s. I remember Dr. Marcus giving him an injection directly into the chest, I guess to try to keep his heart pumping. But the Lord decided he wanted him back that day.

Building

In 1952 Bernice and I purchased a lot and contracted to have a house built on Whittaker Parkway, the first house to be built on Whittaker when the street was still dirt. Our home contained three bedrooms, a living room, a dining room, a kitchen, one bath, and a carport. We had it constructed with brick veneer and trimmed in "Miami Stone" on the front. It had about fourteen hundred square feet of heated area.

The house was still adequate when our second child and first son, Kenneth Earl, was born in 1955. Of course, I was elated to have a son, and I hoped to help him become strong in preparation for his pursuits. Also I was proud to be able to take him around town with me and show him off.

When our third and last child, Karen Denise, was born in 1959, she and her older sister shared a bedroom. As Karen began to grow I saw in her physical appearance a paradox. Her petite size and feminine appearance disguised her athletic abilities and interests. In 1977 we added a large den, a laundry room, a half bath, and a double carport. This is the house in which I still live today.

Searching

For some years following my return home from military service in World War II, I continued to make a living at barbering while constantly staying alert to other opportunities of which I might take advantage. In 1947 I opened my own barbershop by purchasing equipment from John McLendon and renting space from T. K. Bythewood at his Amelia Street funeral-business building. While I was in the army, my uncles John and James Middleton had given me their barber tools. Both these men had barbered at the renowned Herndon's Barber Shop in Atlanta before their retirement.

There were many job and professional positions I was qualified for but could not get because of my skin color. For example, I applied for a job as a mail carrier with the U.S. Postal Service. Considering the years I had spent handling mail during my military years, the question of experience and competence was moot. I took the U.S. Civil Service Commission examination and passed with a high mark. However, that was a dead end. During that era there was one black working at the Orangeburg Post Office, James McPherson.

Another position that was closed to me as a black man, despite my qualifications, was that of stockbroker. I took and passed the examination for a license with the U.S. Securities and Exchange Commission, which qualified me to deal through brokerage firms trading on the New York Stock Exchange. One of the brokerage houses in Augusta, Georgia, an hour and a half's drive from Orangeburg, was advertising for salespeople. I wrote and explained my interest in the position, stating that I had already passed the test for a license. In reply I received a very positive letter from the manager asking me to come to the Augusta offices for an interview. When I arrived there and the receptionist saw the color of my skin, she looked very skeptical and went to get the manager who had sent me the letter. He came to the front of the office, and I told him I was there for our appointment. He denied giving me an appointment. When I produced his letter his reply was, "You may have the letter I wrote, but I didn't give you that appointment my letter to you says you have!" With that he retreated to his office, and the so-called interview was ended. Just like that!

Being a black man in America has not been easy during most of my life. Like others in my family and peer group, I had worked for an education; I had served my country during the war years and received an honorable discharge; I had returned home and married, and now I was trying to find suitable work to earn a living for my growing family. However, qualifications and ability just wouldn't do it for a black man in the segregationist South during those years. The system was rigidly fixed so as not to allow any penetration by blacks.

Still I took advantage of every opportunity I could that would allow me to be of service and add to our family's financial situation. For example, the fact that I had played football in college gave me some experience and knowledge of the game. With this combination I was able to gain work as a referee shortly after Bernice and I were married. To begin with, I worked at the high-school level officiating games. After several years of experience at this level, I passed a written test and gained my credentials to officiate at college games in the Southern Intercollegiate Athletic Conference. Of course, this was part-time work that was seasonal, and I'd call two games a week at most. Many of these games were out of town—for instance, in Savannah, Georgia, or Nashville, Tennessee. T. J. Crawford (now deceased) and William Brown were two other black men I knew who lived in Orangeburg and officiated at games during this time. Also I remember working as a referee with the late A. C. "Chuck" Fields of Columbia, South Carolina, and Isaac "Ike" Washington from Augusta, Georgia. Of course, these referees and all the players in the games they officiated were blacks too, as everything was strictly segregated at the time. It was not until many years later that whites learned black players could carry their teams to victory on the playing fields.

Many fans don't realize the amount of pressure game officials are under. In addition to the normal rivalries and the desire of teams to win, there have always been those whose interest in the winner or loser is great because they have placed bets on the outcome of the games. Officiating can be dangerous too. I have been threatened and even seen other officials physically attacked by those who were disgruntled by their calls and game-related decisions. A habit I developed quickly for road games was to leave town and head home as soon as the game ended. This was a commonsense thing to do, in my opinion. Officiating games was work that I enjoyed tremendously. I probably did it for about fifteen years until my insurance and real estate business grew to the point that it was no longer feasible for me to take that much time away from my family on the weekends.

Chameleon

Because of his run for the presidency of the United States on the Dixiecrat ticket in 1948, his longevity, and the record number of years he served in elective office, J. Strom Thurmond became a national legend. Thurmond's legend lives on after his death. In his home state, South Carolina, almost everyone has a "Strom Thurmond story," and I am no exception.

During the early years of my marriage I had frequent occasions to be on the campus at South Carolina State, where Bernice was teaching. Orangeburg had always been a small town. Being black during those years of segregation meant that we lived most of our day-to-day lives in a small portion of town, which reduced the effective geographic size of our local world even more. The role of the two historically black institutions of higher learning, Claflin and South Carolina State, loomed large in the lives of educated blacks. The schools had many functions, which we attended.

Thurmond was governor of South Carolina from 1947 to 1951. During that time I saw the governor's limousine on the campus at South Carolina State regularly. There was a general understanding that Governor Thurmond was there because his daughter was a student. Of course, at that time South Carolina State was 100 percent black. By his visits Governor Thurmond all but acknowledged having a mulatto daughter.

The young lady graduated and married a law school graduate from South Carolina State. It was said that Thurmond helped him acquire a professional position after the young man received his law degree and that the couple eventually migrated to a western state. Several national publications discussed this situation at least ten years before Thurmond's death on June 26, 2003.

Not because I was a great admirer of Thurmond but more out of a sense of witnessing history and through Joy Barnes's persuasion, I decided to attend the late senator's burial in his hometown of Edgefield. As Joy and I stood in the rain watching the final rites, we invited Phil Lader, former U.S. ambassador to England, to join us in sharing our umbrella. He whispered to us these same sentiments about witnessing history.

About six months after Senator Thurmond passed, Essie Mae Washington Williams, a retired schoolteacher from California, came forward and told the world that she is Thurmond's biracial daughter. Mrs. Williams was encouraged by her children, she said, to do this. She and her immediate family had kept the "secret" about her father because she apparently did not wish to embarrass him. After her revelation she said, "At last I am completely free."

People in South Carolina wondered how Thurmond's white family would react to the public announcement. When he died, the senator had three living children by his second wife, Nancy Moore Thurmond. (His first wife, Jean Crouch, whom he had married when he was in his forties and while he was governor, died about ten years after they married. Many years later he married Nancy Moore, who was young enough to be his granddaughter.) To their credit the family, led by his son Strom Jr., did not deny Mrs. Williams's assertion and apparently met her with some degree of cordiality. In 2005 Mrs. Williams wrote a memoir, *Dear Senator,* recounting her life as Senator Thurmond's daughter by a sixteen-year-old girl who served as a maid in the Thurmond household when her father was in his early twenties.

This kind of situation represents an accepted code of conduct that was perpetuated for centuries in the American South. For many years southern white men in positions of power took advantage of black women. The Thurmond case is a prominent example, and it illustrates one of the many "crosses" black people have been forced to bear. It was in Thurmond's favor that at least he privately acknowledged and supported Mrs. Williams.

I will further add, in Thurmond's favor, that in his later years he acknowledged by his actions that he had changed his perceptions of black inferiority. When he retired at one hundred years of age from service in the U.S. Senate, most blacks seemed to think that his support of and constituent service to black people in the previous forty years or so appeared to be the equal of what he did for whites. It takes a big man to change.

VFW Post 8166

Several years after my return from military service I approached the commander of the local Veterans of Foreign Wars (VFW) about becoming a member. Despite having served overseas, I was not admitted into membership. Although I don't remember being refused specifically because of my race, I didn't need to be "drawn a picture." I'd lived in the South all my life and understood how things like this worked. Those perpetuating the system, while wanting blacks excluded, generally tried to avoid "getting in our faces" about it. It appears to me that this scenario was repeated across the country after World War II. The individual white veterans knew that their black brothers had served honorably and well with them in the war zones. However, in the late 1940s and 1950s the races still were not integrated in many American institutions, especially not in the South. One of the reasons I think some individual white VFW members were sympathetic to our cause was that they cooperated with us when we formed our black VFW posts.

Since the white Orangeburg VFW post was obviously not going to admit black veterans, I saw this as an opportunity to honor a personal friend and former classmate of Bernice's and mine who had lost his life in the war. Some other black Orangeburg veterans and I organized VFW Post 8166 in memory of Broadus James Jamerson Jr., an army veteran. James was killed in the Pacific in December 1943, when an enemy torpedo struck the troop carrier on which he was being transported.

There were seventy-eight charter members of Post 8166. Most of these men were veterans of World War II. They were all personal friends of mine; many of us had grown up together. I have great respect for each one having served in the U.S. Army, Navy, or Marine Corps, and I am proud to have them as brothers in arms. As black men we all had two enemies: foreign foes and discrimination in America. Many of these gentlemen have passed on now.

After their outstanding military service, the charter members of the Veterans of Foreign Wars Post 8166, which was organized on December 11, 1952, made many contributions to the Orangeburg community after their return to civilian life. For that reason I think it is important that they be recognized individually by name (see Appendix 1). This distinguished group of men chose me as their first post commander. At that time Julian Dickenson was the adjutant general, and James W. Cothran was commander in chief.

The location of our first post was on Treadwell Street in the city of Orangeburg. Later we acquired property on Amelia Street that had housed the U.S. Post Office Annex. Post 8166 has been very successful through the years in promoting patriotic activities and providing an environment of fellowship for veterans. In 1990 we had our post "Home Mortgage Burning Celebration." To this day VFW Post 8166 remains vibrant and welcoming to veterans of U.S. conflicts.

Turning a Town into a City

During the days of rigid segregation, black people in Orangeburg learned to create for ourselves a set of social structures that would enhance our lives apart from the white world around us. In addition to the all-black VFW post, we also saw a need to create a private recreational facility for our families. The two main catalysts for change in Orangeburg were Dr. M. Maceo Nance Jr. and Dr. T. Elliott Wannamaker.

Dr. Nance, who became interim president of S.C. State College in 1967 and the school's president in June 1968, had a sense of management and leadership that was evident from the beginning of his employment at State (the shortened name commonly used in conversation to denote South Carolina State College, now South Carolina State University). Nance married Julie Washington, daughter of Julius I. Washington Jr., who served as the business manager at State for a long time. They were the parents of two sons: Maceo, now working with the S.C. Development Commission, and Robert, an aide to Congressman James Clyburn.

In addition to possessing many other assets, Maceo Nance was a visionary. He was not beyond taking business lessons from whites who knew how to turn dreams into realities. He used this talent not only to oversee unprecedented growth, expansions, and improvements at State but also for other endeavors needed within the black community of Orangeburg. One of his efforts in this regard involved Northside Country Club.

A group of black families with an interest in providing wholesome recreation for our children met in the late 1960s at the Sunlight Community Center on Treadwell Street and quietly created our own country club. Nance structured the financing so that memberships were sold as stock shares in the assets. The main asset was the real estate needed for the club's location. Acreage was found about seven miles out on the northwest side of Orangeburg, just off U.S. Highway 178 near Wolfton. The acreage included a lake and a building suitable for a clubhouse. I can't remember if the swimming pool was on the property when we purchased it or if we built it.

We each purchased stock to acquire the property, and members paid dues for the upkeep. There were probably about forty or fifty families involved. It was a nice recreation facility for our young people and a place where wedding receptions, dances, and other activities were regularly held.

Northside Country Club was also an important social institution to have during a critical period in our history. It provided a place to unwind and spend time with our families at a time when much of Orangeburg was closed to us. The club existed until the early 1990s, when members dissolved it and sold the property. By this time almost all facilities in town were open to blacks, and many of us had purchased vacation homes at nearby Lake Marion.

Nance must be given credit as well for larger contributions he made to the prosperity of Orangeburg. When he became president of State, the institution was at a crossroads. The deaths of three college students, shot on the campus by white S.C. Highway Patrolmen in February 1968, created feelings of sadness and outrage that could easily have started the school on a downward spiral. (I will discuss the details of the "Orangeburg Massacre" later in this book.) Nance was interim president when the tragedy occurred and became president a few months later. It became evident early on not only that he was a master at organization and planning but also that he had the people skills necessary to get others to respond in a positive manner.

Historically S.C. State College was the only state-supported institution of higher learning available to blacks. In a state where education ranked at some of the lowest levels nationwide, financial preference had been given to development of the white institutions and their facilities. S.C. State lagged far behind the other state-supported schools in physical plant and adequate salaries for faculty members. Even so, with several thousand students enrolled, it was not only vital in the educational arena but also a socioeconomic powerhouse in Orangeburg.

Nance began by gaining the support of students, faculty, and staff at the college for turning the tide of tragedy into an era of progress for State. He then began to work closely with leaders in the South Carolina legislature who decided on the level of funding for state-supported establishments. He related very well to this group because he was able to anticipate their objections to his proposals for the school and to convince them of the dire need for adequate funding. He used the recent tragedy at the school for a positive purpose. As a result there were more than thirty major construction projects at State—both new buildings and significant additions to existing ones—during his tenure as president, and faculty strength and salaries also increased.

Off the main campus Nance struck a partnership with the city of Orangeburg to build an eighteen-hole golf course on land owned by State close to the city limits. The Hillcrest Recreational Facility has been a reality for many years and is a distinct asset to our city. Further he gained access in the 1970s for blacks to lease some waterfront lots at Lake Marion from the Santee Cooper Public Service Authority. This was a first. His negotiating skills brought more equity in the system of state government resources.

Because of Nance's talents and hard work, many millions of dollars were added to the Orangeburg economy, and this was not a onetime stream of income. State continues to have a major economic impact on Orangeburg's progress each year and is said to have greater influence than any other entity in the city.

Another man responsible for bringing economic progress to Orangeburg is the late Dr. T. Elliott Wannamaker. Having earned a doctorate in chemical engineering from Cornell University, Dr. Wannamaker founded a chemical plant just south of town in 1937. With the advent of World War II the plant manufactured important wartime materials. It grew from there, continuing to diversify its chemical product line according to market demand. In 1953 Dr. Wannamaker sold the plant to Ethyl Corp., a Fortune 500 company headquartered in Richmond, Virginia. Since that time the company has spun off several others, and the original plant is now owned by Albemarle Corporation, an allied company.

Through the years this plant has attracted to Orangeburg a cadre of highly educated scientific workers, mostly chemical engineers, including George Barnes. It has also provided, on average, jobs with higher hourly rates than those of any other employer in town. These jobs came at a time when South Carolina was still making the transition from a largely agrarian economy to an industrial economy. The value of these jobs to a place the size of Orangeburg can hardly be overstated.

Dr. Wannamaker is also well known for his role in founding the private or independent school movement in our state in the 1960s. Apparently these schools were founded to avoid racial integration. While I certainly disagreed with the man on this and a lot of his other political philosophies, he should be recognized for his economic contributions to our area. Through the years the plant he founded has employed many blacks at higher wages than they would have earned elsewhere locally. My good friend Julian Hubert Dean (now deceased) was with this industry almost from the beginning. Julian had a chemistry degree, I believe, and worked in a management capacity. Having twenty or thirty professional engineers in Orangeburg for this long has had an uplifting effect on our progress. In addition to the strengthening of the economy, this plant, like the universities, has brought to town individuals and families with new ways of looking at the way things are done.

Fresh ideas from new residents fuel a desirable kind of growth apart from the obvious economic benefits. In addition to State and Ethyl, Orangeburg has been fortunate during the past several decades to attract other industries and businesses, and this has changed it from a town to a small city during my lifetime. For example, about twenty-five years ago Frank Tourville moved the headquarters of his medical equipment manufacturing company, Zeus Industries, from New Jersey to Orangeburg. Not only did Tourville bring his business, which now includes nine facilities on six campuses (one located in Ireland), but he also brought his family and trusted staff of professionals. Zeus Industries now employs about a thousand people, and Frank Tourville has been one of the most generous people Orangeburg has known in my lifetime.

My friend Bill Cox and his family have also built a significant business in Orangeburg, manufacturing outdoor wooden furniture, lumber, and related products. Cox Wood Preserving is one of the strongest privately held companies in South Carolina. Another friend, Austin Cunningham, a gifted entrepreneur, has contributed immensely to Orangeburg for years, even after retiring from the businesses he brought with him when he moved here.

Although there are other significant enterprises that have strengthened my hometown, I would be remiss if I did not highlight the progress at the institution that is the reason Orangeburg is my home. That, of course, is Claflin University. I've already talked about my family connections to Claflin. Since Dr. Henry N. Tisdale became president in 1994, he has led the university to become among the top institutions in the South. He has accomplished this by strengthening the faculty, constructing and remodeling campus buildings, increasing the endowment fund, and raising the quality of academic offerings. The students have made such strides in their academic accomplishments and postgraduate successes that Claflin University is now recognized as one of the premier liberal arts institutions in the nation.

5

Being My Own Boss

During the 1950s and 1960s I continued to use my barbering skills to earn a living so that I could stay in the South that I loved. As I've mentioned, only a few professions were open in the South to blacks. The white-controlled system kept the doors of opportunity shut on blacks regardless of educational attainment.

Not only did I have this white-dominated system to contend with in my quest to remain an independent businessman, but I also had another insidious element goading me. This criticism came from other blacks. It usually took the form of the question "Earl, why are you cutting hair when you have a college degree and you could be doing something important?" There were a lot of implications in that question. One of these had to do with why I would have spent the money and time to get a college degree and not use it. I had made a choice they didn't understand. Knowing who I am gave me the inner strength to let these implied criticisms roll off my back. I knew my options and where each one could lead. And I never forgot what my idol, I. S. Leevy, had taught me about business ownership being the road to freedom. I knew I had the freedom to do things my salaried friends could not.

It would have been easy for me to become a schoolteacher, which others might have seen as a more appropriate use of my college degree. However, there were several reasons I didn't get into the teaching profession. At that time whites controlled blacks in the educational system. I knew that some of the black people who taught our black students were not qualified, not capable of teaching children. Many blacks who were unqualified went into the teaching profession only to make money. They were officially qualified on paper, but they had to do what the white people running the system wanted them to do, which was mainly to implement social promotions so that our children would appear to be learning when they weren't. I wasn't going to participate in that. It made me sick because I knew that these people were not giving their best and that those controlling the system were not getting the right people to educate our young black people. When I came out of college, I knew I wasn't qualified to teach, and it would have been dishonest for me to take the work and pass young people through my classes when I had not adequately prepared them to advance. Our society is still paying the price today because many within a generation of students graduated from high school only because they were socially promoted.

Also I had decided that I was going into my own business so I could be a free man. For example, I was free to travel around Orangeburg County and organize a committee to establish the first Tuberculosis (TB) Association of Orangeburg County for blacks. I started in North, drove to Livingston in my car, proceeded on to Neeses, and circled around to Branchville and Santee, arriving back home that night. When I came back, I had established names of people who would help with a black TB Association. I could do that because of my independence as a self-employed businessman.

In the late 1950s I became affiliated with the Council on Human Relations. A white lady who was very daring worked with blacks in Clarendon County on the school situation in Charleston. Alice Spearman was her name at that time, and I'll have more to say about her later.

In short I was my own boss this way. I could set my own hours and business habits and had to answer only to my customers in the marketplace. In the years to come, as we fought the civil rights battles, this freedom became even more precious. The value of entrepreneurship should never be underestimated.

All during the 1950s and 1960s I built a loyal clientele at the barbershop. We had a good mix of students, working-class people, and professionals. Ninety-nine percent of my business was from blacks. By showing my customers the advantages of using good products and taking care of their hair with regular shampoos and proper straightening methods, I was able to bring home better than a professional salary. My personality put people at ease and made them comfortable, which resulted in loyal customers.

From the beginning I tried to form good business habits. Our shop maintained regular hours six days a week. The equipment I purchased from Mr. McLendon included four barber chairs. This gave me a chance to offer other men an opportunity to make some money. I encouraged my other barbers to work steady hours also. Usually one or two college students worked with me on Saturdays. It was a good "side hustle" for them to make some money to help with their school expenses. We offered them a percentage based on the work they did, and it was a mutually profitable situation. If I had simply rented them a chair and they had a slow week, it might have put them in the hole. Another habit I established early on was not being greedy in business. For example, as the owner of the shop, I usually had more people asking for me than any other barber when they came in, but frequently I would encourage some of them to let another man cut their hair.

I knew that owning my own business did not mean I could spend the money that came into the cash register each day. In addition to paying my other barbers their splits, there was overhead, including taxes. Forming good habits at the beginning of my business life made things much easier in the years to come as taxes increased and government paperwork and regulations grew in volume and complexity.

Another examination I took successfully around 1960s was to become licensed by the State of South Carolina to broker property and casualty insurance. I could begin work in this field while continuing my barbering. A primary business goal for me was to be in a line of work that would help improve the lives of blacks. For example, owning a pool hall or club wouldn't do that. However, founding an insurance brokerage would help black people protect themselves against unexpected financial disasters. After getting a base established. I took a partner, Eugene A. R. "Skippy" Montgomery, who is now deceased. Skippy and I grew up together and were close friends. He worked full-time as a mail clerk on the railroad. We had not failed to notice that many insurance agencies also brokered real estate. In order to put our company in a position to do likewise, Skippy and I both obtained our real estate brokerage licenses from the State of South Carolina. Blacks went before the same licensing boards as whites did; the process was the same. By establishing a real estate brokerage, we knew we could help increase minority home ownership, which would strengthen black families by helping them build net worth and giving them nice places to live. After some years I bought Montgomery out, and he later established his own insurance agency, which his widow still has today.

Automobile insurance was something everyone needed, and this was what I concentrated on at the beginning. I took the applications in my barbershop between haircuts and shaves. It came to the point that there was so much insurance business I couldn't juggle both. That's when I hired two assistants, Mildred Maple and Margaret Black. They handled the paperwork, and I continued barbering. The business came through my influence in the community. Friends from the educational community, the churches, and organizations to which Bernice and I belonged patronized my business. Frances Mack was another longtime employee during the early years of my business. Mrs. Maple and Mrs. Black both took administrative positions at South Carolina State College when they left our business. Mrs. Mack's husband, Marion, became one of the most successful building contractors in Orangeburg.

In 1964 I purchased from Thomas J. Cade the building located at 211 Amelia Street (which became number 1211 in the late 1990s) across the street from the Bythewood Building and my barbershop. The building was configured for two businesses with two front entrances and a complete division of the space on the interior. I initially purchased the smaller part of the building for the insurance and real estate business, and later I acquired the other side at 209 Amelia as an investment and for the possibility of future business growth. A top-notch interior designer from Columbia was employed to outfit this new acquisition for maximum business advantage.

It took a lot of capital to expand the business in this manner. My best partner in these matters was always Bernice. In addition to taking care of details involved with the children, household management, and getting meals on the table each day, she had a professional salary that was a "sure thing" in the eyes of a bank or lending institution. In addition I still had savings from my craps games winnings on the troop carrier en route to the Pacific in 1945. When I think back on it, since these games included white soldiers as well as blacks, I actually had some white "financiers" during the early stages of building my business.

Throughout my life, even during the days of Jim Crow and segregation and, in fact, as far back as my family's history during slavery, the black Middletons have always known some "good whites" who helped or befriended us. These individuals offset to some degree, in my mind, the system that was designed to hold us down to a certain level because of our skin color. Some will argue that the system was perpetuated by these very same whites. While that could be said, I prefer to focus on the positive traits of every human being with whom I come in contact regardless of skin tones and racial heritage.

In the mid-1960s it became necessary for me to hire a new office assistant. Betty Rush told me she had a sister, Ann Palmer, who was very capable and looking for a job. After Betty phoned her sister and set up an interview, I went to the home of Ann Palmer and her husband, Harry, on Windsor Street. Mrs. Palmer subsequently came to our office for a second interview. After checking her references I made the decision that employing her would be a "good fit" for the work she was seeking and for our business. Still working with us today, Mrs. Palmer, now Mrs. Owens, has been employed at the Middleton companies longer than any other person.

When we discussed Ann's initial employment, she expressed a determined desire to earn her college diploma, which favorably impressed me. After she had been on board for about eight years I encouraged her to go ahead and start her college courses. She took advantage of the fact that we had four-year colleges in Orangeburg and began her studies in business administration. Because my family had impressed on me the importance of education, I felt compelled to fund her tuition and books. After several years she completed the requirements and earned her bachelor's degree from South Carolina State University. By having this advanced education, she has become a much more valuable employee. From a business standpoint, she has more than paid me back for the cost of her education.

Being Prepared

Within a few years following my return from the service I was able to establish a Boy Scout troop, which was sponsored by Trinity United Methodist Church. Of course at that time Boy Scout troops were completely segregated. My experience at Tuskegee had convinced me of the importance of an organization that could help boys learn to become disciplined in a positive atmosphere away from home. On more than one occasion I had seen young men who, I thought, would have lost their way in life if it had not been for their Scout experiences. As far as I know, the troop I established was one of the first in this area for blacks. Maceo Gordon was our assistant scout master.

Our troop met weekly on Wednesday evenings. A large amount of our time was spent working on merit badges. Field trips were a big part of our program. For example, we went to the Fort Jackson army installation in Columbia, forty miles distant from Orangeburg. There the Scouts could witness the drills and routine of army life, which they might experience in the future. Other valuable activities were the overnight camping trips. On these excursions each Scout brought his own food and equipment and cooked in the open. Each outing would begin with a hike to our campsite on Friday evening. This was normally a distance of about ten miles to an area around a church or school, such as St. Stephen United Methodist Church out U.S. Highway 178 North. Because these trips were usually on the weekends when school was out, that meant we were away from church on Sunday mornings. Therefore, we held religious services at our campsite. A nearby pastor or deacon would be asked to conduct Sunday school and the worship hour.

A few of the boys I remember from our Troop 190 were Nicholas Brailey, Johnny Williams, Van Jones, George Winds, Frank DeCosta Jr., Lin Dorman, I. D. Brailey, Samuel Anthony Nimmons, and James R. Lawrence. Altogether we had about twenty-five boys. Of the few I've recalled, Frank DeCosta Jr. became an Eagle Scout.

Being a Boy Scout leader made me feel good because I felt that the Scouting program made a positive difference in the lives of most boys who experienced it. As far as I remember, I "lost" only one Scout in the twenty or more years that I led the troop. One young man was accused and unfortunately convicted by a white judge of being a Peeping Tom, and he died shortly after serving his sentence. I always believed he was innocent. Most of these Boy Scouts went on to have very successful professional careers. And even though some may have migrated out of state, many of them still have strong family ties to the greater Orangeburg community.

This White Lady Deserves a Monument

Mrs. Alice Norwood Spearman was the first white person who befriended Bernice and me after we were married. We met Mrs. Spearman through the Council on Human Relations, of which she ultimately became the director. The council was a group of people throughout South Carolina who were striving to work together across racial lines. Naturally the purpose of the group was not popular with those who favored continued segregation.

Often Mrs. Spearman would have Sunday dinner with Bernice and me when we lived in our first home on Goff Avenue. She was the only white woman I had ever gotten close to at that time. Before that my only contacts with whites had been when I was doing their yard work or other chores for them. She was one of the few white people with whom I could really speak freely and try to discover the differences between blacks and whites. I found that she was just like us. She never tried to act superior around us because she was white, as some others I had been around did, and I could relax during my conversations with her. She believed that blacks and whites are equal. That inspired me to continue to do what I could to promote racial harmony.

We worked together for some years. Mrs. Spearman, I. S. Leevy, and I went to meetings at the Penn Center on St. Helena Island in Beaufort County, South Carolina, south of Charleston. The facility was founded as the Penn School in 1862 by a group of northern missionaries and abolitionists for the purpose of educating newly freed slaves. Until 1948 the school was used for the education of black people. During the civil rights era leaders such as Dr. Martin Luther King Jr. used it for retreats and planning. Today the center is in a National Historic District and is still used for meetings, reunions, and retreats. In the fall of 1959 a Merit Employment Conference was held at Penn. Mrs. Spearman was one of the leaders of the conference, which focused on ways that blacks could gain positions that were being denied based on race.

Mrs. Spearman was a daughter of privilege. She was educated and "married well." If she had so chosen, she could have lived a life of ease and spent her time entertaining, shopping, and traveling. Instead she chose to make a difference. She was hated by a lot of whites, but she was fearless. She knew she was doing the right thing, and their opinions didn't matter to her. She *knew who she was.* Those in the white power structure so despised this fine lady that, during the hearings in Charleston where Thurgood Marshall was arguing for school desegregation, they would not allow her in the courtroom. She had to wait across the street, where people would bring her information as to what was transpiring inside the hearings. Mrs. Spearman reminded me a lot of Eleanor Roosevelt; Mrs. Spearman was an aristocrat, and—like Mrs. Roosevelt—she worked tirelessly for blacks to be treated equally with whites.

Mrs. Spearman's office with the Council on Human Relations was located upstairs in a office building on Washington Street in Columbia, South Carolina. In those days it was a custom in small southern towns to close on Wednesday afternoons and open on Saturday mornings. This was true of my business. I would go to Columbia and visit the Human Relations Office on a lot of Wednesday afternoons. One of those afternoons I was passed on the stairs going up to her office by a stocky young white man running down the steps. When I got to her office Mrs. Spearman was lying on the floor; that man had physically assaulted her. The attack created quite a stir in the building, but fortunately Mrs. Spearman was not seriously injured. She did not want to create a ruckus and, hoping it was an isolated incident, encouraged us to be unaffected by it.

Mrs. Spearman was not a political activist; rather she advised black people on what they could do about voting, organizing, and distributing information on basics such as cleanliness, running water, and education. She encouraged blacks to go where the information was. When it became necessary for her to speak about voting and the advantages, she didn't hesitate to do it. While she was a supporter of the ideals and goals of Martin Luther King Jr., she never was a crusader. She organized and had meetings and gave information and helped the poor. As I think back, she reminds me of the late Mother Teresa.

Later we lost touch with Mrs. Spearman. Recently scholars in the Department of Women's Studies at the University of South Carolina have researched her life and demonstrated the significance of her work to the advancement of race relations in South Carolina. I recently learned that she became a widow in 1962 and married Eugene Wright in 1970. She died in 1989.

To us she was always Mrs. Spearman, an angel in our lives during a very difficult time in our struggle. There should be a monument erected to commemorate her good works and dedication to making the world better for others. It does my heart good to see that the recently published *South Carolina Encyclopedia* includes a biography of Alice Spearman Wright, accompanied by her photograph.

Accommodationist Tactics

My business began to grow during some of the most segregated times in our nation's history. In a small southern town such as Orangeburg that meant most of the financial institutions were owned and controlled by whites. As a businessman I had two choices: one, I could have been bitter and chosen not to deal with whites; or two, I could have been tactful, not sold out my dignity, and used their help as it suited my business needs. I took the second choice because it was more in line with my personality and Christian principles.

Personality-wise I'm more of a cheerleader of people than a critic of how they operate. My religious teachings have been that everyone is the same in God's eyes no matter their skin color; and, if I treat them, as individuals, the way I wish to be treated, hopefully they will reciprocate. I knew that for the system to change, the laws had to change. But beyond that human hearts had to change in regard to the racial situation, and I figured I could influence every white person I dealt with by being mindful of my Christian teachings.

Some of the white leaders who helped me from the beginning of my business included James Walsh; the Council brothers, Charles and Roger; Robert H. Jennings III, the mayor's son; and Frank and Walker Limehouse, my boyhood friends. These men became professionals, business owners, and executives in the Orangeburg lending institutions.

Being an entrepreneur meant that I walked a fine line. Most of my customer base was black, while those controlling the capital markets were white. As a businessman I needed both. My personality and my way of seeing the world allowed me to be successful. By nature I'm a friendly person. I enjoy being with people, and I meet people wherever I go. Who they are makes no difference to me. It's easy for me to deal with almost anyone I come in contact with through my business or community and church activities. Because *I know who I am* it is difficult for another person to insult me or hurt my feelings.

Blacks ordinarily could not get credit at many lending institutions, and I could not take sides with those who were perpetrating this injustice. However, my skin is black, and the fact that they would lend me money meant that this particular wall of discrimination was cracking. So if I succeeded in getting loans and paid them off satisfactorily, this was bound to have a positive influence on whether or not those controlling the system would decide to lend money to the next black person who applied for a loan.

Of course, it behooved me to use credit sparingly during the early years of building my business and particularly not to get "strung out" when race relations became too precarious. This is an example of what I term common sense. I can't overemphasize the part that, through the years, using common sense has played in whatever measure of business success I've achieved.

Statewide Homes Foundation

Trying to use whatever progress I was making to help others was always one of my aims. One of the most valuable assets in a family is widely acknowledged to be home ownership. During the formative years of my real estate company in the 1960s, I joined with a group of black community activists to establish the Statewide Homes Foundation, a nonprofit organization. We had an office at 1523 Harden Street in Columbia.

Our purpose was to find other blacks who were desirous of home ownership and help them make it possible. A lot of education was involved. The first subject we covered was building and maintaining an acceptable credit rating. Then we helped them with the steps to securing a mortgage loan. We taught methods of recording income and expenses so they would be prepared to meet with mortgage loan officers. Qualified contractors were identified in various areas of the state to construct the homes.

Two of the people I remember being involved with in this foundation were the Reverend I. DeQuincey Newman of Columbia and a Reverend Hunter of Florence, South Carolina. All our efforts were through private channels and were not tied in with any government-sponsored programs. Through the efforts of this organization, hundreds of black families across South Carolina became home owners.

A Man of Inspiration

Common sense dictated to me that following the pattern of another successful black entrepreneur increased my chances of success. This is why I. S. Leevy had such an influence on me.

"Given the times in which I. S. Leevy lived and worked, probably no other South Carolina–born African American achieved greater business success nor contributed more to a better life and opportunity for his people," stated the South Carolina Business Hall of Fame video when Leevy was inducted in 1999. Leevy was born into poverty in the Antioch section of Kershaw County in 1876. After attending public schools in Antioch, Mather Academy in Camden, and Hampton Institute in Virginia, he taught school for a year before striking out on his first business venture in Columbia as a tailor and merchant in 1907. In 1910 Leevy married Mary E. Kirkland, also of Kershaw County, and they eventually became the parents of four children. There followed a succession of businesses culminating in a funeral home begun in 1932. Leevy's Funeral Home is still in operation today on Taylor Street and is owned and managed by some of his descendants. Leevy used his businesses as a platform from which to serve his less fortunate black brothers and sisters.

Leevy's positive effect on me has been pervasive my entire adult life. When he was living, I took every available opportunity to be in his company and watch how he "operated." Our relationship was not what I would term "up close and personal." We were not peers; he was close to my father's age. He was, in my eyes, more like an elder statesman, as well as a very successful businessman. I knew he had to have done a lot of things correctly in his lifetime to have achieved what he did. He gave me hope as a black man. Amazingly his great success was accomplished despite the fact that he was blind for the last twenty-six years of his life as a result of glaucoma.

Republican National Convention, 1956

It was partly with the incentive of being in the company of I. S. Leevy that I became a delegate to the Republican National Convention in 1956. Yes, I said Republican. Many people have forgotten that for nearly a hundred years after the Civil War most blacks who could participate in the political process did so in the Republican Party. This is why southern whites voted so solidly Democratic at election time.

I. S. Leevy was affiliated with a group of Republicans who headed up the party in South Carolina. Mrs. John E. Messervy of Charleston was elected as convention president at the May 31, 1956, state convention at the Township Auditorium in Columbia. This state-certified South Carolina Republican Party also elected thirty delegates and alternates to attend the August 1956 Republican National Convention in San Francisco. At the Columbia convention I was elected as one of the South Carolina delegates. The delegation was racially mixed. We traveled to San Francisco via Greyhound bus and stayed at the Manx Hotel.

However, as the convention got under way, it developed that another delegation was also in attendance from South Carolina and claimed to be the legitimate group. This all-white group was headed by David Dows from Aiken, South Carolina. The National Republican Convention's Committee on Contests recommended, and the convention agreed, to seat the Dows-led delegation. This left most of our group as nonparticipants. The main body of our group left on the bus and headed back to South Carolina. However, a few of us decided to stay and see if we could in some way participate in the process. The Reverend. I. DeQuincey Newman was one of those who remained. Those of us who remained were essentially abandoned without return travel arrangements.

I was appointed as an assistant doorkeeper, which at that time carried a remuneration of, I think, about $150. As an assistant door keeper, I witnessed the nomination of Dwight D. Eisenhower to his second term as president of the United States of America. I remember distinctly that one of the seconds to his nomination came from a black female delegate from North Carolina. The main convention proceedings took place at the Cow Palace, a San Francisco landmark.

At the close of the convention I arranged transportation and returned to Orangeburg, I think by airplane via the Columbia Metropolitan Airport. Later some of the people who were left stranded in San Francisco brought suit against the Greyhound Bus Company. Because of the interest that has been expressed in this situation I am including some of the documents relating to it in an addendum to this book (see Appendix 2).

At some point during this time period, in the late 1950s I think, after my attendance at the Republican National Convention, I was informed by W. W. "Duck" Wannamaker, one of the white Republican county officials in Orangeburg and the brother of Dr. T. Elliott Wannamaker, that those in control of the local and state Republican Party would allow no more than 10 percent of their participants to be blacks. That edict was very difficult for me to stomach. Four years later, in 1960, when John F. Kennedy successfully ran for president on the Democratic ticket, I—like the majority of blacks in the country—knew we were welcome in the Democratic Party. I have considered myself a Democrat ever since and was elected on the Democratic ticket during the ten years I served in the South Carolina General Assembly.

Ever since 1960 blacks have voted overwhelmingly for national Democrats. For decades Democrats have pretty much taken the black vote for granted. More and more, however, blacks are asking if the Democratic Party is giving enough consideration to the desires of blacks to ensure our continued loyalty. In my thinking it has about come to the point that if more of us voted for Republican candidates and put Democratic leaders on notice that we must be considered more, we would gain important advantages. Competition generally rewards the groups waging the contests, while those who ask for nothing generally get nothing.

Members of the Orangeburg alumni chapter of Phi Beta Sigma Fraternity during an official ceremony in 1947: (left to right) Wilford Gadson, Dr. Charles Thomas, Hampton D. "Hamp" Smith, Edward Jenkins, Alexander Lewis, unknown gentleman, Jacob Jenkins, Phillip Middleton, Harvin Dash, Earl Middleton, John Gregg, unidentified fraternity representative, Earl Williams, Jimmy Frederick, unidentified fraternity representative, Robert F. Bellinger, James Hall, and James Green. Collection of the author

Some of the original members of VFW Post 8166 at a December 11, 1952, organization event in Orangeburg: (right to left) post commander Earl Middleton, Julius I. Washington III, Matthew "Mackey" Henderson, John Robinson, Thomas E. Haigler, Raysor Adams, unknown member, Clifford Murph, Marion Harrison, Chuck Davis, and an unidentified VFW official. Collection of the author

Earl Middleton's badge from the 1956 Republican National Convention in San Francisco. Photograph by Cecil Williams

Guest pass issued to Earl Middleton at the 1956 Republican National Convention. Photograph by Cecil Williams

Demonstrators on August 23, 1963, marching for the freedom and equality of black Orangeburg citizens. The first six marchers are James Sulton, John Brunson, Earl Middleton, Gloria Rackley, Charles Thomas, and the Reverend I. DeQuincey Newman. Photograph by Cecil Williams

Ella Govan Middleton with her six grown children at an Orangeburg reunion, circa 1975: (seated, left to right) Samuel Thaddeus Middleton, Ella Middleton, and James Walter Middleton; (standing, left to right) Phillip Govan Middleton, Dorothy Louise Middleton, Helen Margaret Middleton Haigler, and Earl Matthew Middleton. Collection of the author

Newspaper photograph of Earl Middleton and his family in 1974, after he was elected one of the first black members of the S.C. General Assembly from Orangeburg County since Reconstruction. Orangeburg Times and Democrat *photograph*

LEGISLATOR'S FAMILY THINKS HE'S 'BEST MAN'—Earl Middleton, the newly elected representative from District 95, has a loyal rooting section, his family. Shown with Middleton and his wife, are from left: Ken, a Furman student; Anita, who is married to Capt. Al Pearson, USA; and Karen, an O-W High student.

I have tried to present my beliefs on the various issues
that are important to our county and state.

If you feel that I can be of service to our county and
state, your vote would be deeply appreciated tomorrow.
In return, I promise to work hard to merit this trust and to
pass on to our state representatives from throughout Sout
Carolina the courtesy and goodwill you have shown me.

LEFT TO RIGHT — Daughter Karen, age 13; Earl Middleton; son
Kenneth, age 17; wife Bernice; mother Mrs. Ella G. Middleton who has
lived in Orangeburg for 90 years. Absent from this picture is the oldest
daughter, Anita Louise Pearson, age 25, wife of Capt. Alphonso Pearson
stationed at Fort Campbell, Kentucky.

VOTE MIDDLETON FOR THE HOUSE OF REPRESENTA

Poster used in Earl Middleton's campaign for the S.C. House of Representatives in 1974. In the photograph (left to right) are Karen Middleton, Earl Middleton, Ken Middleton, Bernice Bryant Middleton, and Ella Govan Middleton. Collection of the author

The Reverend Jesse Jackson in 1980 at the South Carolina State House, speaking for the reelection of President Jimmy Carter. Representative Earl Middleton is just to the right of the podium. John Harper, a well-known community activist, stands to the left. Collection of the author

Earl Middleton shaking hands with Vice President Walter Mondale, Charleston Air Force Base, March 1980. Collection of the author

The first formally organized S.C. Legislative Black Caucus meeting with Benedict College president Henry Ponder (first row, right) in 1975. First row: I. S. Leevy Johnson (Richland County District #74) and Juanita Goggins (York #49); second row: Robert R. Woods (Charleston #109), Joseph Murray (Charleston #111), Kay Patterson (Richland #73), and McKinley Washington (Charleston #116); third row: George Wilson (Richland #81), Theo W. Mitchell (Greenville #23), and Ernest Finney (Sumter #70); fourth row: John W. Matthews Jr. (Orangeburg #94), Hudson Lee Barksdale (Spartanburg #31), Earl Middleton (Orangeburg #95), and B. J. Gordon (Williamsburg #101). Collection of the author

The S.C. Legislative Black Caucus, circa 1982: (left to right) Kay Patterson, John W. Matthews Jr., Julius Murray, Theo W. Mitchell, I. S. Leevy Johnson, Earl Middleton, Juanita White, B. J. Gordon, Hudson Lee Barksdale, Larry Blanding, McKinley Washington Jr., Joseph R. Murray, and Robert R. Woods. Collection of the author

Members of the S.C. House of Representatives at their desks in 1983. Representative Earl Middleton appears front and center. S.C. House of Representatives photograph

Representative Earl Middleton introducing family and friends in April 1984, after announcing his plans to run for the S.C. Senate in District 40: (left to right) campaign manager Fred Broughton, brother Samuel T. Middleton; grandson Jarae K. Middleton, held by his father, Kenneth E. Middleton; wife, Bernice Bryant Middleton; sister-in-law Verona W. Middleton; sister Dorothy Louise Middleton; and daughter-in-law Cynthia Bonnett Middleton. Photograph by Cecil Williams

Part Three

Serving the Cause

6

Overcoming the System

As in the entire nation, the victories of the civil rights movement in Orangeburg County, South Carolina, did not come cheaply or quickly. Unfortunately Orangeburg paid the ultimate price before the upheaval ended. It would be good for me to discuss some of the events dating back more than a hundred years that contributed to the February 1968 deaths of our three students in Orangeburg. Their sacrifices have been overshadowed in the pages of history by the assassination of our nation's civil rights leader fewer than sixty days later.

Orangeburg in some ways is typical of any southern town, and in other ways it's unique. The town was named for William, Prince of Orange; its original street names come from some of the members of His Majesty's Council, hinting at the English influences in this part of the country that are embedded in our subconscious. (My own surname, Middleton, is a glaring example.) These influences were brought across the Atlantic, sometimes by way of Barbados, by the soon-to-be owners of large plantations and human chattel. The ownership of other humans was vital to ensuring the wealth and easing the lives of this small, so-called aristocratic group of planters.

It took a civil war to free black people from this yoke of unpaid bondage. At this point in our history there was a dawn of hope for our newly freed ancestors. For example, my grandfather Abram Middleton was a delegate to the 1868 South Carolina Constitutional Convention in Charleston, the output of which is still acknowledged by historians as a superior document. He purchased acreage and became a home owner. Abram and our family could finally worship without fear of reprisals. He used his educational skills to such an exceptional degree that he was chosen to serve as one of the inaugural trustees of Claflin University, which was established to educate newly freed slaves. Blacks were also enrolled at the University of South Carolina. There was a great anticipation that blacks would finally be allowed to work and live in an environment free of fear. However, those in power never relinquish it easily. The Civil War may have ended, but southern whites were not through fighting.

Around 1876, through an organized campaign of terror and fear, Wade Hampton and his followers in South Carolina began a systematic drive to wrest from freedmen their hard-won rights. These whites could not conceive of living as equals with their former chattel. Similar to those in other southern states, this malicious South Carolina group reversed what had been accomplished in a decade of progress by newly freed blacks. This destruction of rights continued into the twentieth century with hard-core segregation and the resulting Jim Crow laws, which I experienced firsthand from my youth onward.

The monumental 1954 Supreme Court decision in *Brown v. Board of Education* was the dividing point in my lifetime as far as blacks' freedoms were concerned. This decision opened the possibilities for black people in this country to begin participating in basic aspects of American life, such as being able to vote, accessing a decent education, and using public accommodations, which whites had always had at their disposal. However, between the possibility and the actuality of blacks being given equal treatment, a lot of obstacles still had to be overcome.

Earlier I described the predicaments blacks faced using the public buses in Montgomery, Alabama, where I was stationed during World War II. According to the established rules that whites in control of the system had in place, blacks entered through the back doors of the buses and rode in the back. In addition a black person was always required to yield his or her seat to a white person. One day, about a year after the *Brown v. Board of Education* ruling, a tired black lady, Rosa Parks, who had worked all day at her job as a seamstress, refused to yield her seat on a Montgomery bus to a white man. Ms. Parks's refusal to be treated as less than she was sparked the Montgomery bus boycott and resulting protests in favor of equal rights for blacks.

At about this same time in other parts of the South, blacks were beginning to protest unequal treatment. In Orangeburg we were in the middle of demonstrations designed to "level the playing field" of life between blacks and whites. Of course the NAACP was at the forefront of this initiative. Since Orangeburg had a large cadre of blacks with higher-education degrees, we were pioneers in leading these pro-civil-rights activities. It was also at this time that we began hearing about a young black minister in Montgomery, the Reverend Doctor Martin Luther King Jr. He was rising as a leader by organizing peaceful demonstrations in protest of the horrendously unequal treatment of blacks.

I went back to Montgomery in 1955 to attend a huge rally and Sunday meeting that we heard Dr. King was organizing at Dexter Street Baptist Church. The Montgomery bus boycott had just started. Two other black Orangeburg businessmen, Leroy Sulton and Julius I. Washington III, also attended. Sulton and his brother James owned an Esso service station on Russell Street next to where South Carolina State University's Bulldog Football Stadium stands today. Washington owned a poultry business near his residence just off College Avenue. Our traveling trio was an example of that lesson I. S. Leevy taught me about the independence entrepreneurship gave one. Sulton, Washington, and I were our own bosses. If anything happened to prevent us from getting back to Orangeburg by Monday morning to work, there was no one to fire us.

Sulton had a brand new 1955 Buick Century automobile that he wanted to try on the road, so he drove. We left Orangeburg at midnight on Saturday and drove straight through, arriving in Montgomery close to daybreak. We found the home of Ralph David Abernathy, one of Dr. King's assistants, and knocked on his door. After he admitted us we slept on his living room floor for a short time. I'll never forget the fact that his phone continually rang with harassing and threatening calls.

Abernathy told us that for his own protection he didn't own a car. If he drove a car he owned, someone could purposely run into him or easily single him out for attack; or he could be hauled into court for a trumped-up traffic violation. Worse yet, a bomb could be planted under his hood.

During the rally at Dexter Street Baptist Church, people were "hanging from the rafters" because there was such a crowd there to hear Dr. King. We were called on to relate the progress of our Orangeburg Movement, which was chronologically ahead of the one in Alabama, to our Alabama brothers and sisters. Then Dr. King spoke. He was still in his twenties and just getting started as a national leader. His genius was already obvious. By late Sunday night we were back in Orangeburg. The weekend excursion had enriched our lives.

The Orangeburg Movement

The *Orangeburg Movement* is the term used to describe the mid-twentieth-century civil rights struggle in Orangeburg, South Carolina. The movement began in the summer of 1955 with a petition to Orangeburg School District 5 officials from black parents asking that our children be allowed to attend the schools nearest their homes. The movement ended in 1968 with the Orangeburg Massacre.

In our city local black citizens, including students, staged sit-ins and protest marches, which resulted in mass arrests. Black people were astute enough to know that the more widespread the arrests became, the more ridiculous the white power structure would look in the eyes of the nation and the world. As a result, changes to the system would come more quickly. My wife, Bernice, was steadfast in her determination to participate. She gladly allowed herself to be arrested on September 28, 1963, for picketing in front of Kress & Co. on Russell Street in downtown Orangeburg to protest their segregated lunch counter. Her group was carted off to the state penitentiary in Columbia, where they were put in the dungeon! When she came home several days later, she told me of the many indignities they had been subjected to. Kenny, then eight years old, distinctly remembered that when his mother returned to Orangeburg her lips were chapped and swollen; there had been no toiletries or grooming supplies in the penitentiary. While his mother was gone, he stood forlornly in the driveway of our yard looking for her and wondering when she would return.

When our peaceful demonstrators were arrested we had to go through legal channels to have them freed from jails and prisons. A young black attorney named Matthew J. Perry, now a distinguished federal judge, was one of those at the forefront of the legal process in this area, along with attorneys Ernest Finney Jr., now retired chief justice of the S.C. Supreme Court; Zack Townsend; Earl W. Coblyn; and W. Newton Pough. Posting bail was a part of that procedure. Since I was in the insurance business, I was also a bondsman and was prepared to bail our people out of jail, and I did that on many occasions. This work also tied into my responsibilities as a member of the S.C. Advisory Committee to the U.S. Civil Rights Commission.

Those in control of the system gave us hell! They did every kind of thing imaginable to keep us from being treated equally. A lot of those people are dead now, and some of them have descendants still living in Orangeburg. I'm not going to name any names because I'd almost prefer to forget. But I do intend to mention some of the good whites who have always been around to help.

My best boyhood friend, Alex Lewis, and his family were treated by some whites in a way that was really inhumane; I can't think of a better

word to describe it. Alex and I finished Claflin together and were fraternity brothers. Like me, he served in the U.S. Armed Forces during World
War II. Also like me and many other returning servicemen at the end of
the war, he married his childhood sweetheart, Alba Myers. She and Bernice were both highly intellectual, obtained the highest education degrees
in their chosen fields, were professors at South Carolina State University
for many years while they were raising families, and retired from the university after long and distinguished careers. Alex's father, Lemuel C.
Lewis, was a contractor and master bricklayer, as skilled at masonry as
any man whose work I've seen. Alex went to work with his dad after the
war and eventually came to own the business after his father retired and
passed away.

In 1955, when black people in Orangeburg began petitioning and
writing letters to the white school officials asking that black children be
admitted to the public schools closest to their homes, some of the more
demented whites decided to take reprisals against blacks who signed the
petitions. My friend Alex and his family got a double dose.

Unlike the businesses I owned, which were patronized almost exclusively by blacks, Alex subcontracted a large portion of his work from one
prominent white building contractor. When Alex signed the petition, that
mean-spirited individual cut off all Alex's work. Alex was forced to leave
town to find employment to support his family. When I drive by that white
contractor's house today, where his son now lives, there is a Confederate
flag prominently displayed. Although the man who gave my friend hell is
dead now, every time I drive by and see that Confederate flag it reminds
me of how hateful he was to my friend.

That was not the end of the reprisals that the whites in control of the
system in Orangeburg had in store for my friend. Alex and Alba had one
son, Mickey, who was a few years older than our son, Kenny. When
Mickey was fairly young he was diagnosed with hemophilia. This is a
hereditary condition in which one of the normal blood-clotting factors is
absent; as a result prolonged bleeding can be caused by even minor cuts
or bruises. Mickey had a severe case and required regular and sophisticated medical care involving medications and blood transfusions. Local
representatives of the medical establishment threatened to deny Mickey
medical help if Alex signed the petition. That was inhumane. At one point
Alex had to carry his son to New York for medical care.

Fortunately there were several white medical professionals, real humans, in Orangeburg who made it known that they would help the Lewises. Dr. James C. Shecut (now deceased) was one. Dr. Shecut's family,

which included several generations of physicians, had migrated to Orangeburg from Charleston. His dedication to making sure that Mickey got care was so great that, in order to avoid getting tangled up with those controlling the medical system, Dr. Shecut kept the lifesaving blood Mickey needed at home in the Shecut family refrigerator. When Mickey needed blood the doctor called his wife, and Mrs. Shecut removed the blood from the refrigerator so that it would be the proper temperature for transfusion into Mickey's body.

Other white Orangeburg medical professionals who helped the Lewises were R. Sumpter Williams Sr. and his son R. Sumpter Jr., owners of Orangeburg Pharmacy. They continually provided medicines needed to keep Mickey alive.

I cannot overstate the importance of what the Shecuts and the Williamses did for the Lewis family at that time. The white community put pressure on each and every one of their peers to withhold any essentials needed by black citizens in Orangeburg. That a few blacks might die as a result was something some of them hoped for to "teach the niggers a lesson."

Partly as a result of a few good whites doing what they were supposed to do, Mickey Lewis grew to manhood. He graduated from college and earned his master's degree. He married and had a daughter. Eventually he became an administrator at Clemson University, and he was working at California Polytechnic Institute in California when he died at forty years of age in 1989. Mickey's daughter, Amber, graduated from Clemson University and also earned her master's degree.

It is easier for me to remember the good whites who helped than those who tried to crush us at that point in Orangeburg's history. In fact, I try to forget the hatefulness, and this helps me not to become bitter. Today Mrs. R. Sumpter (Mary) Williams Jr. is one of Orangeburg's grand ladies. An octogenarian, she is still active in our community and doing benevolent work every day. She carries forward the spirit of love for all people, regardless of their skin color, that her husband and his father demonstrated during their lifetimes.

During the civil rights era people of color by the thousands were threatened and harassed as whites who controlled the system continued to try to deny basic rights to us. The example I've just related about the Alex Lewis family is one with which I am familiar. Many other individual stories could be cited.

During that time we continued to meet in the evening at Trinity Methodist Church, headquarters of the Orangeburg Movement, to get reports from people out in the field, set up our next operation, protest continuing injustices, and plan marches in front of segregated businesses in the nonviolent manner advocated by Dr. Martin Luther King Jr. I could see from my local experience that, by going about our work for equality in the peaceful manner that Dr. King encouraged, we saved our country from a far, far worse situation than we experienced in the 1960s.

Because my wife was a college professor, we made friends with many people who also aspired to higher education. When they wanted to work on advanced degrees, unless they went to Atlanta University or maybe Howard, they always had to go north to enroll. For example, Bernice did advanced graduate work at the University of Pittsburgh in Pennsylvania. Blacks were not allowed to enroll in graduate schools at white southern universities, and most of the black institutions of higher learning did not have graduate schools. Advanced educational opportunities were denied to blacks by the white southern institutions on a systematic basis with almost no exceptions.

The indignities of segregation were constant. We were not allowed to use public facilities such as libraries, water fountains, or rest rooms. If Bernice and her friends went shopping, they could purchase clothes in some stores but were not allowed to try them on even though white customers were permitted to do so. The same was true of hats and shoes. The ordinary functions of day-to-day life were roadblocked by court rulings and segregationist laws until well into the 1960s. In addition, despite the cadre of highly educated blacks who populated Orangeburg because of their positions at our two historically black universities, Orangeburg lagged far behind in implementing blacks' rights once they became law. For instance, in 1964, TEN YEARS AFTER the *Brown v. Board of Education* decision was handed down by the U.S. Supreme Court, Orangeburg's public schools still were not integrated. Black citizens in Orangeburg banded together under the auspices of our local chapter of the NAACP and the Orangeburg Movement to bring this basic access to education to our children.

Because I was an independent businessman, no white person could fire me from my job, so I became the signatory on some of the correspondence to the superintendent of the Orangeburg city schools insisting that our children be allowed to enroll in the public school nearest their homes. Of course, the officials continued to drag their feet and put us off. We had to get legal help from Matthew Perry.

Many people were deeply involved in the Orangeburg Movement, including attorney Earl Corblyn, Dr. Charles Thomas, the Reverend

I. DeQuincey Newman, Isaac Williams, John Brunson, James Sulton, and John Robinson. Two people who could be called leaders of the movement were the Reverend Matthew D. McCollom and Mrs. Gloria Rackley De Journet. Bernice has called Gloria "Miss Movement." According to Bernice, "Gloria was a teacher in the Orangeburg school system and was fired for her involvement [in the Orangeburg Movement]. Her two daughters were also involved. A brilliant woman."

Bernice has also cited the *Torch* (also known as the *Flaming Journal of Freedom*) as being instrumental in the movement. Volume 1, number 1, of the *Torch* is dated August 28, 1963. Charles Cottingham, a professor in the Department of Natural Sciences at South Carolina State College, was editor of the publication, which was printed on a mimeograph machine. Some issues were only two pages, printed back and front.

Cecil Williams—a well-known and respected Orangeburg photographer who chronicled the civil rights movement with his camera—has called the *Torch* "a sort of an underground thing. It kept us up to date on who was going to jail and who was getting out and was pretty comprehensive." The *Torch* was mainly distributed at mass meetings during the heart of the movement. According to Williams, the newsletter was published for about a year, and there are very few issues now in existence. The April 30, 1964, issue was number 23.

The movement was very well organized and was generated by young people with adult leadership. Students at S.C. State and Claflin as well as high-school students played vital roles. The first strategy of the Orangeburg Movement was to boycott certain white-owned local businesses to demonstrate the economic muscle of black buying dollars. This "selective buying campaign" was initiated in the late summer of 1955 and was very effective. It was started because blacks in the movement were subjected to economic pressure. In some cases they were fired. In other cases Orangeburg businesses cut off their credit. The boycott was organized to the extent that we took buses to Columbia every Saturday so people could shop there instead of in Orangeburg.

Another strategy was the picket line, which was also well organized. Meals were served at Trinity Methodist Church (now Trinity United Methodist Church). The all-white Orangeburg police force, at the behest of the white "city fathers," did everything in their power to break up the picketing. New ordinances appeared overnight. One required that a person had to have a permit to picket; another one said that picketers had to walk in single file.

These peaceful demonstrations were very effective strategies. The demonstrations eventually led to mass arrests. The police always over-reacted by using fire hoses and other unnecessary force. At the peak of the movement they had jailed so many students that they were using the county jail, the city jail, the armory, the chain gang camps, and even the Central Correctional Institution in Columbia, which is where Bernice was taken.

One of the S.C. State students participating in the demonstrations, a boy named GiGi Zimmerman, was a midget. With the fire hoses in use by the local officials at full blast, this young man was almost washed into a sewer drain. Only the bars over the opening of the hole saved him from going in and being drowned. The white officials couldn't have cared less.

Things were explosively tense and kept building. For instance, for transportation the police used the penitentiary bus, and on one occasion they even brought in a cattle truck to take students to Columbia. Some of the kids were arrested two or three times or more, including our daughter Anita. Mostly from black middle-class Orangeburg families, these young-sters saw firsthand the effects of segregation on the lives of their loved ones and themselves. They were determined to do their part actively to change things. And they did.

In 1963 Anita turned sixteen. She and others in her age range, spent most of the year in and out of jail for marching, sit-ins, and picketing. They were arrested time and again. When this occurred, the "authorities" separated the juveniles from the adults before taking them to penal facili-ties. Anita and her group were always taken to the Orangeburg county jail on St. John Street. The jail, which was commonly referred to as "The Pink Palace" because of its color, was built by Jonathan Lucas in 1860. Union general William T. Sherman used the jail for his headquarters in 1865 and burned it as he left Orangeburg. However, Lucas rebuilt the partially de-stroyed jail in 1867. It was remodeled in 1921 and used as a jail until 1980.

There were many, many people not on the forefront who made their contributions in other ways. For example, Alma McPherson and Lillie Matthews, along with other women, were in charge of serving meals to the demonstrators. I don't know how they got the food, but they produced balanced meals. There were others who gave money and didn't want to be identified for fear of losing their jobs, including some who were employed as teachers. A very small, naive minority said they couldn't understand

what the activists were fighting for, and there were others who were
fearful of getting involved, but the majority of black people were really
together. It was a classic example of unity, of what unity can do, of what
unity can achieve. Regrettably, though, this was not the end of the struggle for racial freedom in Orangeburg.

Claflin College (now University) played an integral role in the Orangeburg Movement. As a private institution, Claflin at certain times had
advantages that South Carolina State could not claim. Ultimately South
Carolina State was controlled by whites. As a state-funded college, it had
to go to the almost all-white South Carolina legislature each year for budget approval. In addition, as well as I remember, many of State's trustees
at that time were white men. So State was on a tightrope when it was time
to fight for civil rights for black people. When Dr. Martin Luther King Jr.
came to Orangeburg to speak in 1967, he made Claflin College and Trinity Methodist Church his "headquarters." His visit to our town was a
highlight of the Orangeburg Movement.

By 1968 one of the remaining businesses refusing to allow blacks to
purchase its services was the All Star Bowling Lanes on Russell Street in
downtown Orangeburg, about three blocks from South Carolina State
and Claflin. Because bowling was one of my hobbies, I was involved with
trying to negotiate an agreement with the owner, Harry Floyd, for use of
the lanes by black people as well as his white patrons.

In the early 1960s a group of black men in Orangeburg had formed a
bowling team. The team consisted of Lamar Dawkins, a businessman;
Burns Wilson, a professor at S.C. State; Dr. Oscar Butler, an administrator at S.C. State; Sergeant Carney, an ROTC instructor at S.C. State; and
myself. Because we were not permitted to use the local bowling alley, we
drove back and forth to Columbia, forty-five miles away, for our weekly
matches. Our team was serious and skillful and won several trophies.

In connection with our personal interest and participation in bowling,
we approached Mr. Floyd in the fall of 1967 to ask about our team and
other blacks using his facility. Since the time we had organized our bowling team and before we met with Mr. Floyd, the U.S. Congress had enacted civil rights laws that apparently covered businesses such as bowling
alleys. We took this into consideration before our meeting with him.

Mr. Floyd ostensibly had nothing against black people, but he used
the argument that if he allowed blacks in his bowling alley his white
customers would refuse to come and thus put him out of business. He
claimed that his business was not covered by the public accommodations

section of the civil rights laws as it was local and no interstate commerce was involved.

Of course some black college students were also interested in bowling at this location, which was close to the campuses of Claflin and S.C. State. After some weeks progress in negotiating with the owner slowed to a snail's pace, and the students became impatient. We met with Orangeburg mayor Edward O. Pendarvis and officials of the Orangeburg Chamber of Commerce in an effort to rectify the situation.

Not being admitted to the bowling alley was another racial rebuff in a string of incidents that blacks had experienced for decades. This time the students were not going to let it go by unaddressed. They began picketing in front of the bowling alley to protest. They continued to try to gain admittance and were refused. The situation escalated as more students joined the protest. The students were anxious and exuberant. College officials met with students in order to calm them down, but these meetings did not have the desired effect. As the students walked from the bowling lanes back to their campuses, they were angry at being denied admission and allegedly began to damage property along the way, breaking store windows and damaging vehicles. Governor Robert E. McNair felt compelled to call out the National Guard to ensure order in Orangeburg. It was very frustrating to everyone involved, and nerves were frayed. The tension mounted.

On the evening of February 8, 1968, after we had our family dinner at home with the children, Bernice and I went to my office on Amelia Street. While we were there, I received a telephone call letting me know that the students were out of control on the S.C. State campus despite the presence of armed National Guardsmen across the street. Bernice and I drove to the campus, which was less than a mile northeast. Because I had been serving as a member of the S.C. Advisory Committee to the U.S. Commission on Civil Rights, my purpose was to gather information for a report to the commission. Earlier that day I had called the Washington headquarters and advised them that the situation in Orangeburg was on the verge of erupting and that urgent action was needed. It appears that federal authorities were prevented from getting help to us because it wasn't clear if the All Star Bowling Lanes legally came under the public accommodations section of the civil rights laws. This dilemma remained unresolved.

Across College Avenue from the campus, Bernice and I could see the National Guardsmen and S.C. Highway Patrolmen with their weapons.

As we approached the entrance, we saw students on the hills to the left
and right of the driveway. Someone in the crowd threw a brick and broke
a headlight on my car. We did not stop until we reached Lowman Hall,
about a hundred yards past the entrance on the right.

Bernice saw one of her students, and we slowed as she addressed him.
"Hey, Smitty, come here!," she called to him. As he approached the car we
could see that he had empty Coke bottles in his hip pockets and one in
each hand. When she asked him what he was doing, he attempted to tell
her the plan the students had for fighting back that night. Bernice tried to
discourage him by emphasizing that the National Guard troops and Highway Patrolmen armed with guns were just across the railroad tracks and
waiting for the protesters to make a move. He ignored her advice and
proceeded toward the College Avenue campus entrance. As we drove on
I inquired, "Who was that young man, Bernice?" She replied, "Henry
Smith." At the time the name was not one I knew. A few hours changed
that. Since there was no purpose for our remaining on the campus, we
went home.

Later that evening we heard gunfire from the direction of the campus
a mile away. An acquaintance in that area called with information that
students had been hit by gunfire and taken to the hospital. I drove to the
hospital, which was then on Carolina Avenue, and saw ambulances delivering people, seemingly students, who were obviously in emergency condition. Because there was nothing I could do to help, I returned home. My
official assignment was to observe and report.

My family and I did not get much sleep that night for fear of what had
taken place. Within our household we did not fear for our own personal
safety. However, we knew what historically had happened to blacks when
they had gone against the system.

The next morning we found out that our worst fears had come true.
Three S.C. State students lay dead: Henry E. Smith, Samuel Hammond Jr.,
and Delano H. Middleton (no kin). They had been shot on the campus by
patrolmen who had allegedly been firing from across the street.

These deaths were completely unnecessary. Not long afterward a federal judge ordered the bowling alley to desegregate. Whites bowled in lanes
next to black bowlers, and this was not an issue.

More than a year after the killings, nine patrolmen were tried, and
all were found not guilty in the deaths of the three students. The jury,
seated in Florence, South Carolina, was composed of ten whites and two
blacks. The only person ever convicted in relationship to the Orangeburg

Massacre was a young black man named Cleveland Sellers, from nearby Denmark, South Carolina. He was convicted on trumped-up charges of allegedly inciting a riot. He served a prison term of less than one year and was later pardoned. Sellers later earned his master's degree from Harvard and also a doctorate. He now serves as director of the African American Studies Program at the University of South Carolina. His son, Bakari, a law student, won a seat in the S.C. General Assembly in 2006. S.C. Republican governor Mark Sanford, who was elected in 2002, has since officially apologized on behalf of the state for the students' deaths in 1968.

The year 1968 continued as one of monumental tragedy in our country. Dr. Martin Luther King Jr. was assassinated on April fourth of that year in Memphis, Tennessee. Further tragedy struck when Senator Robert Kennedy, a national friend to black people and a presidential candidate, was shot in Los Angeles on June fifth and died the next day.

I. S. Leevy, another person of great significance in my life, also passed away in 1968. More than any other person I encountered outside my family during my formative years, he provided me with a clear vision for my life as an ambitious black man.

Cancer

Early in 1963 the Good Master reminded me who the boss is. Some warning signs in my general abdominal area sent me to the offices of Doctors L. P. Thackston Sr. and Jr. and Neil C. Price. Dr. Thackston Sr. was regarded as one of the preeminent urologists in the country. Fortunately, he was located in Orangeburg.

Following tests I returned to his office at the Urological Institute for the results. They were not good. Dr. Thackston explained that the tests showed a malignant lesion on my bladder. The doctors said they could not give me a prognosis, but they gave me two sheets of paper and told me to follow the instructions on them.

Cancer is never a welcome companion. Its victims know it never comes at a convenient time. This was certainly true for me. Our third child, Karen, was only four years old; Kenny was eight and a third-grade student; and Nita was starting high school. Mama was devastated. In 1963 the advances in treating malignancies were not nearly as sophisticated as they are today. A diagnosis of cancer was still akin to a death sentence. Once stricken, an individual could only remain optimistic, pray, and try to engage a top-notch physician. We did all of these and enlisted help with the prayers. As Dr. Thackston called the shots on my medical treatment plan, Mama, Bernice, and other members of my family—along with many friends—went to work on the prayers. Mama and one of her friends, Elizabeth Hook, conducted a three-day prayer fast on my behalf.

On the doctors' instructions, I went back to the Urological Institute on Carolina Avenue, where Dr. Thackston operated and removed the growth. As I was coming out of the anesthesia I heard one of the doctors tell the other, "I believe we've got a miracle here." That statement filled me with hope. In the weeks and months ahead the sensations in my bladder disappeared. Since 1963 I've had regular checkups, and fortunately I've had a clean bill of health in that regard.

Selective Service Board

In 1965 I was chosen to serve on the Selective Service Board for Orangeburg County. Of course, I was the only black on the board, and probably the first. Throughout the country blacks were extremely underrepresented on local draft boards at that time. In 1967 there were only 261 blacks on boards nationwide, or 1.5 percent of the total number. Eventually the good-thinking white people of Orangeburg began to see, however, that institutions were stronger if black people were part of the decision-making processes.

At that time the Vietnam War was raging, and American males were still subject to being drafted. The job of the Selective Service Boards was to classify males according to their priority to be called for active duty, usually in the army. Certain factors were taken into account, such as educational status, physical condition, and support of certain family members.

Young men with the 1-A classification were subject to being called at any time. Members of the board had an obligation to be meticulously fair and level-headed. Another board member who served when I did and who was conscientious in his duties was Macon Garrick, a businessman. Since his death Garrick's sons have carried on his retail furniture store with great success. For eight years, until the draft was ended in 1973, I served on the Selective Service Board of Orangeburg County. During much of this same period the Orangeburg Movement was ongoing.

Earl Middleton in 1968 with his secretaries Sheila White and Ann Smalls Palmer Owens at the Middleton Agency on 211 Amelia Street. Collection of the author

Middleton Agency joins largest brokerage firm

By MAURA COUCH
T&D Business Writer

The Middleton Agency Inc. has joined the nation's largest real estate brokerage company, becoming its first black-owned affiliate.

According to an announcement made Thursday at a meeting of the Orangeburg County Board of Realtors, the 39-year-old Orangeburg real estate firm is now an independently owned and operated member of the Los Angeles-based Coldwell Banker Residential Affiliates Inc. Coldwell Banker operates approximately 1,400 offices nationwide.

The new affiliation will be reflected throughout the Orangeburg area on the new blue and white signs: Coldwell Banker Middleton and Associates, Realtors. The new signs will appear on real estate that is for sale or lease, said Earl Middleton, owner of the local firm.

Coldwell Banker is owned by Sears, Roebuck and Co. The nationwide real estate company is a member of the Sears Financial Network along with Sears-owned Dean Witter Reynolds and Allstate Insurance.

"As a member of Coldwell Banker, The Middleton Agency becomes part of a 78-year-old company that offers the most complete and professional service available in the United States," Middleton told area Realtors.

The biggest advantage of being a Coldwell Banker member is the Sears connection, said William J. Minus, a Coldwell Banker representative.

"Members can offer benefits no one else in the business can. For example, their buyers receive a number of discounts at any Sears store on items related to their home purchase," Minus said.

Coldwell Banker is in the process of expanding across the United States into cities with populations below 500,000 through its affiliates program. Currently only 12 Coldwell

Signs tell story

Kenneth Middleton (left), sales manager of the Middleton Agency, and Earl Middleton, owner, display the sign indicating the firm's new affiliation with Coldwell Banker, the nation's largest real estate brokerage company. (T&D photo by Ken Tyler)

Banker offices are located in South Carolina.

"Since Orangeburg is a growth area, Coldwell Banker had been looking for an individual company to represent them. We were told they chose us not because we're minority-owned but because they were looking for a top broker to represent them, said Kenneth E. Middleton, the local firm's sales manager. "And with us, Coldwell Banker is assured of good solid professionalism," he said.

Earl Middleton said Coldwell Banker covers all aspects of the residential marketplace. It owns Nationwide Relocation Service, whose membership consists of more than 700 real

estate firms throughout the country.

It also owns Coldwell Banker Relocation Management Services, one of the nation's largest corporate relocation home buying companies, as well as Previews, Inc. and Homes International Magazine, companies specializing in the worldwide marketing of luxury properties, he said.

"All of these connections represent opportunities for us to better serve our clients. Coldwell Banker offers us separate know-how, vast resources and a more visible national image to enable us to provide the finest and most complete spectrum of real estate services," Ken Middleton said.

Newspaper article announcing Coldwell Banker's selection of the Middleton Agency as one of its affiliates. In the photograph Ken and Earl Middleton show one of their new yard signs. Photograph by Ken Tyler, Orangeburg Times and Democrat

Earl Middleton visiting a monument dedicated to the Tuskegee Airmen, May 1997, Walterboro, South Carolina. Photograph by Kenneth E. Middleton

Earl and Bernice Middleton at the 1994 Coldwell Banker Middleton and Associates Realtors annual awards banquet in Orangeburg. They are holding a photographic collage of the company's business associates. The original was presented to Bernice in appreciation for her behind-the-scenes support through the years. Photograph by Mitchell's Photography

Coldwell Banker Middleton and Associates Realtors at the January 1994 awards banquet, Corson Hall, Claflin University. At this annual event the company's top Realtor receives the Earl M. Middleton Award, which Ken named in honor of his father. Collection of the author

Earl Middleton and John Kluge at the carriage house on Kluge's Morven Farm estate, near Charlottesville, Virginia, 1996. Photograph by George R. Barnes

Earl Middleton and Edmund Fishburne Bellinger Jr. in front of a painting of one of Bellinger's great-grandfathers, probably Joseph Bellinger, the father of Edmund Cussings Bellinger. Photograph by Joy W. Barnes

Phillip, Earl, and Kenneth Middleton in September 2001 at the Country Club of Orangeburg. Earl is holding a citation naming him Kiwanis Club of Orangeburg Citizen of the Year. Photograph by Dr. Eugene Atkinson

EARL MIDDLETON—*TRUSTEE EMERITUS*—

NOVEMBER

2003

IN APPRECIATION FOR YEARS OF DEDICATED SERVICE
AS A TRUSTEE OF THE MIDDLETON PLACE FOUNDATION

Trustees of Middleton Place Foundation in November 2003, the year Earl Middleton became a trustee emeritus: (kneeling, left to right) June Duell Waterman, Stuart Dawson, Caroline Duell, Holland Duell, Pierre Manigault, and Frank Middleton; (standing, left to right) James Ferguson, Earl Middleton, Charles Duell, Rutledge Young, Ken Middleton, Jane Hanahan, Tom Chrystie, and Heyward Carter. Collection of the author

The Middleton family in Charleston after the May 29, 2004, dedication of a historic marker celebrating accomplishments of the Middleton family. Photograph courtesy of Al Pearson

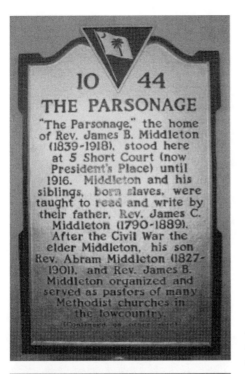

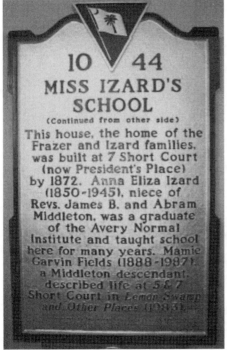

Historic marker (front and back) honoring black Middletons, between the 5 and 7 President's Place properties in Charleston. Photograph by Joy W. Barnes

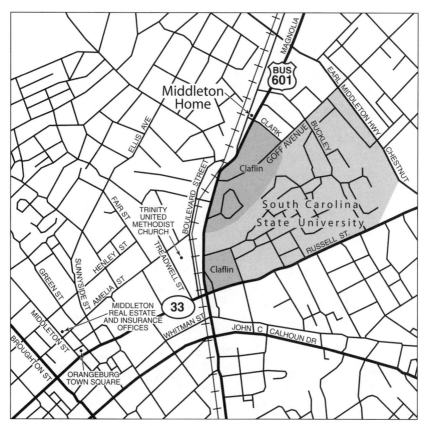

Map showing a portion of the city of Orangeburg, which has changed little since the 1920s and 1930s, when Earl Middleton was growing up. The Middleton home was on Clark Street just west of Magnolia Street. Map by Judy Burress

To Earl Middleton
With best wishes,

President George W. Bush presenting the Congressional Gold Medal to Tuskegee Airman Earl Middleton at Charleston Air Force Base on July 24, 2007. White House photograph by Eric Draper

Decade of Progress

Encouragement

At the end of the 1960s the federal civil rights laws that had been enacted and the changing mood in the nation once again gave blacks the possibility of wide participation in the political process. By this time I had been involved in many phases of activity both locally and on a statewide basis. Many individuals and groups, black and white, were encouraging me to seek public office. It had become obvious to me that others considered my willingness to listen to them, my years of participation in church and community service, and my personal attributes to be what they wanted in a public servant.

Even though some friendly whites had said positive things to me about seeking office, I was realistic enough to understand that at election time it was still a "race game." I considered the fact that the number of blacks registered to vote in our state had grown from 58,000 in 1958 to 220,000 in 1970. By this time blacks voted mostly for Democrats and were participating to some extent in party affairs. The South Carolina delegation to the 1968 Democratic National Convention included a significant number of blacks. In 1970, for the first time since the 1890s, three blacks were elected to the S.C. General Assembly—Herbert U. Fielding of Charleston County and James L. Felder and I. S. Leevy Johnson of Richland County. Johnson, a Columbia attorney, was the grandson and namesake of the man I wanted to emulate, I. S. Leevy.

Still the racial makeup of the S.C. Senate and House of Representatives districts made the election of a black person unlikely. Each county had a state senator, and most House districts were apportioned so that whites were in the majority. Then, through reapportionment decisions, the federal courts began slowing dismantling the white power bases. The S.C. Senate was reapportioned several times between 1967 and 1972. Each time an improvement was made in the fairness of the racial percentages in the given districts. These favorable changes were occurring as I was attaining a secure plateau in my business after a quarter-century of serious, steady work. My family was doing well, and it became possible for me to consider running for office.

The election of the three blacks to the S.C. House in 1970 was very encouraging to me. In 1972, after continued encouragement from people I respected, I decided to offer for a seat in the S.C. House of Representatives from Orangeburg. At this time we had three seats in Orangeburg County, and all candidates ran at large throughout the county. The contest was still decided in the Democratic primary in Orangeburg County.

My supporters and I ran a serious campaign throughout the county. My candidacy received much backing from the black community and a tiny bit from whites. These supporters worked tirelessly for my election, and they gave their money too. The campaign treasury received monetary contributions from hundreds of individuals and groups in all areas of Orangeburg County. Some contributed more than one hundred dollars, while others gave one dollar. By careful budgeting we utilized every dollar to the maximum.

On election night the question of my success turned into a cliff-hanger. When all the votes were tabulated, I had lost by a slim margin. Even so, my supporters were encouraged. They were not excited because Earl Middleton had almost won; rather they were heartened because a black person they trusted had almost been elected for the first time in a hundred years.

Strengthening the Business

In addition to a change in the political arena I sensed a transformation in my Orangeburg business associations about this time. Orangeburg real estate company owners all operated autonomously. There was the Orangeburg Board of Realtors but no multiple-listing service. When a prospective buyer wished to purchase a house, he or she found it necessary to go to almost every company in town that had property for sale. The brokers had no formal agreements showing and selling houses listed with other companies. If another company had a house listed for sale and I was working with a prospective buyer who was interested in it, I had to get

permission from the listing broker to help sell that property. Listing brokers had a habit of picking and choosing among those who wanted to see
a property and those who wanted to sell it. Of course, race entered into
this, but money mattered more. Some brokers perceived that they could
pocket the entire commission if they didn't have to split it with another
company, and the prospective buyers were forced to come to them to deal
on the property. It is pretty obvious that this system worked to the detri-
ment of both buyers and sellers.

Up to this point black real estate brokers had a national organization,
the National Association of Real Estate Brokers, to which I belonged. Our
counterpart was the largely white National Association of Realtors. This
segregated situation existed with almost all black professional groups in
the country. As soon as I sensed the wind shifting in business, I approached
Roy Krell, a Realtor in the eastern part of Orangeburg County, and asked
if he would support me for an at-large membership in the National Association of Realtors. With such a membership I could gain the advantage
of belonging to the largest organization of real estate professionals in the
world, and the local group would not be confronted with an integration
issue that they might not want to face. To be honest I didn't think they'd
let me in, but the advantages made it worth my while to try.

Roy Krell was the developer of a new resort at Lake Marion, about
twenty miles east of the city of Orangeburg, and he was an official with
the Orangeburg Board of Realtors. He seemed approachable and friendly.
Above all he seemed to be a businessman. Krell was receptive to my idea,
and to my astonishment I was admitted to membership in the local group
representing the National Association of Realtors. I definitely felt that this
membership opened up some new marketing possibilities for me.

As a part of my business philosophy I had always tried to project a
sense of presence in the community. I never intended for my business to
remain segregated forever. We maintained appropriate ads in the Yellow
Pages of the phone directory and the local newspaper, the *Times and
Democrat*. In addition, I was out in the community on a daily basis making personal contacts.

During the 1960s, in tandem with passage of the civil rights laws,
some other programs were put into effect to try to alleviate the economic imbalance that appeared to exist for blacks and some whites. One
of these was an initiative toward home ownership. This 235 Program was
administered by the Federal Housing Administration (FHA), which later
evolved into the Department of Housing and Urban Development. Under
the 235 Program individuals and families earning less than a stipulated

income could apply for approval to receive a loan to purchase a home and have their payments subsidized. There was also a significant reduction of the conventional down payment. This initiative became known as "low-income housing."

The program was very popular, particularly in Orangeburg County. Entire subdivisions were constructed by builders knowing there would be a big demand. And there was. Qualifying was easy, and a purchaser was not required to put down much cash. Hundreds of these houses were constructed and sold in Orangeburg County. However, a problem arose when it became obvious that most of these purchasers were not prepared to handle the responsibilities of home ownership. They did not under-stand the importance of maintaining and keeping up their property. Many also lacked the financial knowledge and skills to make their payments in a timely way. As a result, a large percentage of these homes were re-possessed. Once these repossessions occurred, the FHA had to secure the services of local brokers to manage these vacant properties. Real estate brokers submitted bids in an attempt to get the contracts. Fortunately my company won the bid, and the Middleton Agency became the FHA-VA broker for an area covering Barnwell, Bamberg, Orangeburg, and Cal-houn counties.

As time passed, the number of repossessions increased dramatically, and at times we were responsible for the management and security of as many as a hundred houses. Becoming an FHA-VA broker raised the pro-file of the Middleton Agency. Therefore, it was no surprise when I received a telephone inquiry in 1970 from a young, white female agent at another broker's office on the possibility of cooperating brokerage on some "235" lot sales. Mrs. Joy Barnes, a white woman, subsequently came to my office, and we previewed the lots. During the next couple of years we stayed in touch on an infrequent basis, mostly at Realtor meetings.

It had always been my desire to build an integrated business if the opportunity presented itself. I could envision profitability in diversity that could not be brought about otherwise. My experience in the military and the limited but successful individual relationships my family had with whites, even during the most segregated times in our history, gave me this notion. An integrated business would also help increase minority home ownership by expanding the range of locations where homes could be purchased.

Probably the most dramatic change in my business began in 1972, when Joy Barnes returned to my office and asked for a position as a real estate agent. At first I had misgivings about hiring her. As I told a *Wall Street Journal* reporter twenty years later, "I was afraid to hire her, afraid to ride in a car with her for fear that whites would think I wanted to rape her." However, I decided to think about the decision from a business standpoint. Joy had a degree from Clemson University and was working on her master's at South Carolina State University at the time. She seemed to be able to relate to different kinds of people and communicated well. The fact that her husband also had a real estate license to bring to my business influenced my decision as well. I agreed to bring her onboard.

Exactly as I had anticipated, Joy opened up a completely new stream of contacts for my business. She belonged to a different church than I; her husband, George, was employed as a chemical engineer at a Fortune 500 company plant in Orangeburg, and they had a different set of social contacts in our community. In real estate brokerage a diffusion of contacts is the lifeblood of profitability.

In the span of four years between 1968 and 1972 I could see the racial landscape in my life changing. After the three black students lost their lives, it seemed to dawn on most people in our town that we could not allow a tragedy of this nature to happen again. The Orangeburg Board of Realtors had admitted me to full membership; I had come very close to being the first black in almost a hundred years to be elected to the S.C. House of Representatives from Orangeburg County; and my business had become integrated with the addition of George and Joy Barnes as licensed real estate agents.

Northwood Estates

About this same time another door, with a nice portfolio of business, opened for my company. Two brothers and businessmen from Columbia, Thomas and Ralph Bagnal, had come to Orangeburg and acquired acreage on the edge of town off U.S. 301 north going toward Santee. In the early 1970s they started constructing approximately thirty single family houses on this land. The Bagnals owned a building supply company, which they sold only within the past few years. At the time these houses, which were part of Northwood Estates, were upscale for Orangeburg. All were of brick veneer construction, measured approximately fifteen hundred square feet or larger, and had a minimum of three bedrooms and two baths; most also had garages. As developers, the Bagnals got the streets in the subdivision paved and put in a system to handle the sewerage. Water was already accessible to the area.

Not only was the project begun with a well-developed plan, but also, very important to me, the location chosen for their project was in a "racially neutral area." Historically housing patterns had developed in Orangeburg along racial lines; black people lived in all-black neighborhoods, and whites lived in all-white neighborhoods. Of course, we didn't know it at the time, but this was about to change.

In the early part of the 1900s blacks had migrated north in droves. That's where the decent jobs were, and skin color made less difference in that area. Making money and turning a profit for a business owner mattered more in the North than did the race of the person holding the job. Many blacks who had gone north made good salaries and built retirement incomes; for example, they worked at blue-collar jobs such as the Port Authority in New York or the railroads in Chicago or the phone company in New Jersey. By the early 1970s many were ready to retire and wanted to move back "home" to the South of their youth. At about the same time that the Northwood development came into being, blacks in significant numbers began returning to Orangeburg and other areas in the South.

Until that point, because of the racial demographics as well as the way neighborhood housing patterns had developed in Orangeburg, the only homes for sale more than 90 percent of the time were those in white neighborhoods. Blacks generally built homes and lived there until the husband and wife both died. Then the children inherited the property and live in the houses. In addition, blacks had not moved into technical and management positions in large numbers yet. Thus there were few job transfers among blacks; jobs occupied by blacks stayed local for the most part. These two factors ensured that there was virtually zero turnover in black neighborhoods. There were a few exceptions—for example, when a college professor would move to Orangeburg or army ROTC instructors at State College would move in and out. When blacks from out of town (or even the occasional local) wanted to purchase houses, we almost always had to show them homes in white neighborhoods. Some blacks were not comfortable with this.

I got acquainted with the Bagnal brothers as Northwood was well under way but before the first house had sold. They became confident that I could get the job done for them, *and* the color of my skin did not bother these gentlemen. We agreed that my company would handle the marketing for the Bagnals' large, quality business. Our sales efforts were very successful because of the pent-up demand I have just described. It worked well for the Bagnals too, as I remember, for when I got a house under contract they would finish it while the closing was being processed. This also helped the buyers as they were able to select finishing materials such as cabinet colors, wallpaper, and countertops.

The blacks returning to Orangeburg from the North understood that it takes money to purchase a home or do business. This is something that many in the South still haven't learned, not even today. When these people, many of whom I had known years before, began to come to our company to purchase homes they had their down payments ready, and many even paid cash.

In addition to the fact that my sister Dorothy Louise, my daughter and son-in-law Anita and Al Pearson, and my son, Kenny, were all home purchasers in this neighborhood, Bernice and I were able to make a sizable investment there too. We were able to purchase eight partially finished houses, which I personally completed for rentals to others and which I still own today. Since I used my free time after office hours and on weekends and put my own sweat equity into the project, it turned out to be a good investment. Here again some of my peers expressed the opinion that I was wasting time using my college degree to paint houses. However, I remembered that in part I had earned my degree by working with my brothers to build a home on Claflin's campus. I didn't mind getting my hands dirty, and I certainly didn't mind having income from those rentals each month. If I had used that leisure time to attend out-of-town ball games or had a wife who insisted on social activities as a hobby, that would have dictated a different outcome—and a different income.

Northwood Estates is still one of the nicer upper-middle-class neighborhoods in our city. It is a personal example for me of what opportunity and hard work can do to help people and also create a profit. An increase in local minority home ownership took a significant jump when this neighborhood was completed.

Elected

In 1974 the South Carolina legislature reapportioned the S.C. House of Representatives into 124 single-member districts based on population. This fact—combined with the close race we had run in 1972—encouraged me to try again for election to the State House. We ran a campaign that was organized similarly to the one in 1972, and this time we were successful. The difference was that the lines of the House districts were much more equitably drawn.

Much of the credit for bringing about these positive changes in House reapportionment in South Carolina goes to attorney Armand Derfner of Charleston, who led a private group of lawyers based at that time in

Washington, D.C. Their the legal work on the South Carolina reapportionment case resulted in single-member districts for the S.C. House of Representatives. As a result thirteen blacks were elected to the House that year. Also elected from Orangeburg County in 1974 was another black man, John Matthews, a public-school official from Bowman. Today he serves in the S.C. Senate.

From the beginning of my service in the legislature I felt that the office belonged to the people of House District 95. It was my responsibility to listen to them and, as nearly as possible, to represent their wishes. Although the percentage of blacks in the district was slightly more than the percentage of whites, I let it be known right away that I was colorblind in this regard and would be representing all the people. Also, I felt an obligation to make an attempt to keep my constituents informed as to the business that was being transacted on their behalf each week at the State House in Columbia.

It was suggested that I write a weekly report to the people in the local Orangeburg newspaper, the *Times and Democrat*. This idea appealed to me, but I was skeptical about the paper's willingness to accept my articles for publication. After some urging, and knowing that the reports would be a good service for citizens in District 95, I reluctantly approached the reporter who handled governmental affairs. I will never forget the positive reaction I got from Marv Caughman. He too thought that it was an excellent idea and agreed that my reports could appear in the Sunday edition for those weeks during the year when the General Assembly was in session. Mr. Caughman's progressive attitude was backed up by his editor and publisher, Dean Livingston.

The implications of this agreement may not seem significant to the average person. However, black people, historically, were not used to being treated fairly by the media, or in any other arena of American life. For that reason, even though race relations had advanced by 1975, it was still not the norm for a white person in authority to agree *willingly* to give a black man serious exposure in the press, particularly the first black in a hundred years to occupy the legislative seat I held.

As in most towns, the local newspaper is an important institution. The *Times and Democrat* began in 1881 with the merger of two papers that had in turn been formed by the merger of several others. Like most publications in the South during Reconstruction, the Orangeburg newspapers were embroiled in political doctrines. James L. Sims, a Charleston native, was one of the original principals in the merger that formed the *Times and Democrat*. The paper remained in the possession of the Sims family until

Howard Publications acquired total ownership in 1981. Lee Enterprises acquired Howard Publications and subsequently the *Times and Democrat* in 2002. Cathy Hughes is the present publisher of this newspaper, which has a history of never missing a scheduled publication in spite of a devastating fire in 1972, a crippling snowstorm in 1973, and a catastrophic hurricane (Hugo) in 1989.

Throughout the years that I served in the legislature, the *Times and Democrat* published our "District 95 Report" on a regular basis. In my opinion the paper has continuously been fair in its coverage of race-related issues through the years since.

During my legislative years the opportunities for service increased significantly. I relished this part of the work. It was also a great learning experience that I wish more people could have. I'd like to share some of what I encountered and observed during my years in elective office.

The first legislative session in which I served started in January 1975. This just happened to be a year in which we had a new governor taking office. He was Dr. James B. Edwards, an oral surgeon from Charleston with strong Orangeburg ties. Dr. Edwards was the first Republican governor to be elected in South Carolina in modern times, the first in nearly a hundred years.

Immediately following the gubernatorial inauguration and lunch, the House of Representative went back into session. Representative I. S. Leevy Johnson took the podium and called to our attention the fact that it was Dr. Martin Luther King Jr.'s birthday, January fifteenth. This was an example of how blacks could finally put to the forefront some issues important to us. Two weeks later we were successful in getting through the House and Senate a concurrent resolution paying tribute to Dr. King. Being able, after such a long period, to get official recognition for a matter of concern to minorities was encouraging to many. It gave me a good feeling at the beginning of my legislative career and made me more determined than ever to be conscious of representing everyone in my legislative district regardless of color.

The Speaker of the House of Representatives at that time, Rex Carter, named me to the House Labor, Commerce and Industry Committee. Representative Clyde Dangerfield, a Charleston businessman, served as committee chairman. Within this committee structure I was made chairman of the Real Estate Subcommittee, a position I held during my entire time in the legislature.

One of the most high-profile pieces of legislation in years was before the South Carolina legislature in 1975—the Equal Rights Amendment to the United States Constitution. Because a majority of the people in Orangeburg House District 95 appeared to support this amendment, I did too. The intent was to put women in the workplace on an equal economic footing with men. However, House members who opposed the measure were astute enough one legislative day to call for a vote immediately after lunch when they saw that they had the votes to defeat it. This came about because some members were a few minutes late returning from the lunch break. South Carolina never approved this amendment. In my opinion, this is an outstanding example of why our great state continues to lag behind in many economic, social, and educational measures—there's a collective state of mind that's resistant to positive change.

Proposed laws concerning every imaginable area governed by the state come before lawmakers each term. Some proposals are for repeal of laws already in effect. Some important issues that affect our citizens, such as education, were the focus of attention a quarter-century ago and are just as important today. During my first term there were legislative proposals relating to public-school discipline and teacher retirement.

Each year the legislature must approve expenditures itemized in the state budget bill. Some years reaching consensus on passing the budget bill is easier to accomplish than others. Going through the state-budgeting process each year made it easier for me to see how government can become too powerful and flagrant with taxpayers' dollars. There's only one source of revenue to fund government entities, and that's the people. It can come directly from taxation or fees; it can come from taxes on higher earnings by individuals and corporations; it can come in the form of higher prices on goods and services that have been taxed; it can come from taxes on property owned; and now in South Carolina it can come from our state government acting as a bookie and encouraging our citizens to gamble.

It is generally acknowledged that the people who can least afford it purchase lottery tickets. In South Carolina one way the gambling interests got the legislature to make the lottery legal was to label it an "Education Lottery," with some portion of the money supposedly going to help solve our state's dismal education rankings. In fact, our state will go further in the hole by having to help pay for the essentials for those who spend their meager incomes on lottery tickets.

In the yearly legislative budget process, state agencies and their administrators who want additional funding definitely have an advantage over taxpayers who want their taxes held down. Here's why. Individual taxpayers, whether on others' payrolls or working at their own businesses, must spend their workdays earning their wages or profit. They can't spend two days a week at the state capitol lobbying their lawmakers to lower taxes or at least not to raise them. However, heads of state agencies can spend their days lobbying to get their funds increased, and they get their paychecks while they are doing it! Not only is this not fair; it's also not right. I must give our present governor, Republican Mark Sanford, credit for recognizing and trying to do something about this.

So what's an ordinary citizen supposed to do? The answer is stay alert. Take an interest in what's happening in your community. Know the educational situation in your area. Familiarize yourself with the state of health care. Know where the money is generated in your town and state. Read the news everyday. Keep up with what's happening at all levels of government. Be aware. Initiate political conversations with your peers. Talk to your lawmakers and write letters and send e-mails to them. See them personally when they attend events in your area. Tell them what you think. Most are interested in doing what the greatest number of voters want done because they want you to reelect them. And most of all VOTE! Vote in every election. Don't ever think you're too busy to vote. Our polls are open from 7:00 A.M. to 7:00 P.M.; plan on it. Even if it's absolutely impossible for you to get to the polls, that's still no excuse; you can get an absentee ballot.

Unbeknownst to most people, there is a very important way to give your input to state lawmakers. During my years in the South Carolina legislature, I learned that public hearings are held on most proposed bills or laws. Usually these hearings are conducted by legislative committees or subcommittees. Generally you must make your desire to be heard known ahead of time to committee personnel so they can plan for space and time allotments.

Probably one of the quickest ways to become acquainted with the elements of local and state government structuring is to peruse the government sections in the local or Columbia phone book. There is a toll-free telephone number, 800-922-1539, for obtaining information about any bill before state lawmakers for consideration. It was implemented the first year I served in the South Carolina House and is still in effect. Other states surely have similar setups. All these details about the inner workings of government may seem tedious and boring, but being aware is the price we must pay for the right to our way of life. Freedom is not free!

During the first three years of my legislative service, a bill to reinstate the death penalty in South Carolina hung over lawmakers. It was generally acknowledged that public sentiment was overwhelmingly in favor of once again adding this ultimate penalty to the repertoire of judicial sentencing possibilities. As an individual, I have always opposed the death penalty on moral and religious grounds. One should not have the right to take a life because only God can give a life.

By chance I missed the actual vote on the death penalty bill. It came on the same early summer afternoon in 1977 that our son, Kenny, graduated from Furman University in Greenville, South Carolina. It was one of the few votes I missed in ten years. The measure passed, and the death penalty has been in effect in our state ever since. However, I did manage to make a statement for the official record that if I had been present my vote would have been against reinstatement.

At the beginning of my attendance at legislative sessions in Columbia, I made an important observation. As a black member of the legislature I was treated exactly like the white members as far as appointments, invitations, and other considerations were concerned, and I was almost always treated with courtesy by everyone. In my estimation the positive dynamics resulted at least partly from the fact that no two members of the House were competing for the same constituency. As representatives from single-member districts we felt free to help each other while we interacted in Columbia. We felt a kinship with one another as in a fraternity or sorority.

Many of the past ways of doing things were changing during my early years in the legislature. In many ways what was happening in South Carolina reflected events throughout the country. As more opportunities became open to blacks without the usual fights of the past to gain every inch, the "old order" began to retire. For example, in 1975 the Edgar O. Brown State Office Building was dedicated to the long-serving former state senator known as the "Bishop of Barnwell." An aging man at this time, Brown was present at the dedication to receive accolades. Still serving as a House member at the time was Speaker Emeritus Solomon Blatt of Barnwell County, which had also been home to my families' former owners. We served together in the House for several years before he retired. Senator L. Marion Gressette from neighboring Calhoun County was near the end of his almost fifty years of service in the S.C. Senate during my early years in the House. These three gentlemen, all from small rural counties, basically controlled what happened in South Carolina for several decades before the advent of home rule and the reapportioning of the General Assembly.

To their credit I must say that these leaders were polite and treated me with respect during their remaining years in the legislature. In fact, one of the highlights to me individually was a gathering that Speaker Blatt held at Barnwell State Park during my first term in the House. As I recall, of 124 members he invited a group of about 25 to discuss some legislation. He included me in the group. My relationship with these gentlemen who represented the ways of the past reflected my relationship with most other members. I think it said a lot about their willingness to change and acknowledge what they knew was correct even if they had not considered it possible before.

Realtor of the Year

Near the end of my first term in the legislature I received the unexpected and pleasant honor of being voted Realtor of the Year by my peers on the Orangeburg County Board of Realtors. They seemed to be genuinely proud of the fact that one of their members had attained the position of chairman of the House Real Estate Subcommittee for the entire state of South Carolina.

Within the industry at that time Orangeburg Realtors were not known for welcoming newcomers to their ranks. Several years before, when my membership in the Board of Realtors was accepted, my being black would certainly have been an official excuse for not admitting me and my company. That this did not happen spoke more highly of this group than the reputation they bore. In hindsight, I believe that Lois Lengal, a Realtor at the Harley and Cuttino Company, had a lot to do with encouraging other members to choose me as Realtor of the Year.

One of the most significant things to me about being honored with that title was the fact that the vote had been taken by individual secret ballots of the members. Except for me there might have been, at the most, two other black members of the Orangeburg Realtors and possibly none. This meant that a majority of these white professionals could see that race made no difference and accomplishments did. In a southern town such as Orangeburg at that time in our history, the importance of this realization and resulting action by a group of working professionals cannot be overestimated.

Mama

One morning about dawn in late January 1976 my sister Helen Haigler called to let me know that Mama wasn't doing well. Mama had lived with Helen for some years after we all agreed that at her advanced age she should no longer live in our Clark Street home, even with a boarder. That day the legislature was in session, but I had not yet left for the drive to

Columbia. I went right over to Helen's home, and she in the meantime called Dr. Raymond O'Cain.

Dr. O'Cain had been Mama's physician for a long time, as Dr. Green had passed on years before. A white doctor, O'Cain was held in high esteem in the black community because he treated everyone the same. At his office there was only one waiting area for patients. There were none of those signs with the word *Colored* and the red arrow underneath pointing to another room—usual for the times even in the 1960s and 1970s. During this same time Bernice and I had to take Karen, our youngest daughter, to Florence, South Carolina, an hour's drive from Orangeburg, to the nearest orthodontist who would treat black patients. This gives an idea of why Dr. O'Cain was so loved by the many blacks he served.

As I remember, there wasn't a lot Dr. O'Cain could do for Mama that morning. She had high blood pressure and heart disease. At over ninety-five years of age she couldn't pull through another winter. Of course, it's always sad to lose your mother, but when a black man comes into the world that's the only person he knows for sure he has in his corner. We could really celebrate Mama's life because she had done so much for so many—I mean people she didn't *have to* help but helped anyway.

As one of the first graduates of South Carolina State College, she taught hundreds of children in the years before she and Papa married. She nurtured her own six natural-born children, seeing to it that we all earned college degrees. In addition, she raised the Brower daughters in our home. In those days before the advent of widespread, effective birth control and with an adult life expectancy that was only around forty-five years, there were always unwanted and orphaned children who were in desperate need. In addition to her usual church and community work Mama did her best for such people when she knew they had no one else.

She set an example, and we strove to pattern ourselves after her. I think that's the highest tribute people can pay to their parents to try to follow their example—in our case a caring, Christian person's example. When we buried her next to Papa at the Orangeburg Cemetery three days later, her floral tributes included one from the governor of our state.

Legislation

During the years I was privileged to serve in the South Carolina legislature, I was able to introduce some ideas through the sponsorship of bills to represent the wishes of ordinary citizens. In 1978 I initiated successful legislation that eased the yearly hassle motorists had endure as they stood in line for hours to renew their automobile license tags. Previous to that time everyone's tag expired on the same date every year. By designing legislation that required the South Carolina Highway Department to stagger the expiration dates throughout the year, we were able to prevent the long lines people had previously been forced to endure.

Another measure was designed to cut down on the annual legislative production of new laws. At that point approximately seven hundred to eight hundred new laws a year were going on the books in South Carolina. My proposal called for a committee to study the feasibility of stopping the introduction of new legislation after February fifteenth, except for the appropriations bill, for the 1980 session. Further, each standing committee would have been required to study all existing laws and repeal those that were no longer necessary. Reducing the number of frivolous lawsuits was the purpose of another measure I sponsored.

Of course, proposals such as these involved more common sense than legal brilliance. I suppose it depended on how one looked at the position. Some members of the S.C. General Assembly saw themselves as lawmakers or legislators, meaning that they saw their primary function as grinding out new laws to go on the books. I saw myself as a representative, being there to act according to the wishes of my constituents. That doesn't necessarily mean putting more laws into effect. My years in business have taught me that government must be very careful not to hamstring our citizens with unnecessary laws and regulations. If an injustice needs correcting, that's a different matter, of course.

The Legislative Black Caucus

The year I began serving in the legislature there were 12 other black persons elected to the S.C. House of Representatives. There were still no black state senators. However, we 13 could get some things accomplished from a prospective that had been absent for nearly a hundred years. Although 13 of a total House membership of 124 may not seem like many in terms of a percentage, that number gave us a voice that could be heard. We did not have the votes to get a measure passed, but the opportunity to be heard and to go directly to the people of South Carolina was a refreshing change. In addition, there was a peer group who could meet and discuss the unique dilemmas of blacks in our state. We often found that even though a white House member might be empathetic with struggles that were largely associated with blacks, whites were often hesitant to initiate actions to deal with certain situations. They didn't want to be seen by blacks as getting involved in matters that didn't affect them primarily, and they didn't want to be seen by whites as doing more for blacks.

This situation led to the formation of a caucus by the black House members. *Caucus* is defined as "a private meeting . . . of a political party or faction to decide on policy, pick candidates . . . esp. prior to a general, open meeting." The main purpose of the South Carolina Legislative Black Caucus was to ensure that black citizens in South Carolina had a voice in the legislature. For example, the caucus was able to bring about a speaking engagement by a civil rights leader before a joint assembly of lawmakers for the first time in the history of the state legislature. In the spring of 1976 Vernon Jordan Jr., head of the National Urban League, spoke at the State House in Columbia. In addition, he was entertained at the governor's mansion and shown such warm hospitality in the capital city that he subsequently wrote a newspaper article about his visit.

It's unlikely that a group of white lawmakers would have invited Jordan or anyone in his position; they never had before. I'm convinced that it was some whites' first exposure to a black man of national prominence, who was educated and well mannered, spoke correctly, and was impeccably dressed. Jordan's visit did a lot to bring blacks and whites together psychologically. He is a role model for black leaders, and I wish there were more like him. When Jordan walks into a room he makes a positive impression, and when he speaks he makes an even more positive impression. Even today, as he pursues a lucrative law practice in our nation's capital, plays golf with a U.S. president, and serves on corporate boards, he is an example of a black man who casts a positive light on our race.

Of course, Jordan was not the only black person to appear before the legislature. The Legislative Black Caucus created an awareness of black citizens that had not previously existed within the elective body. In 1977, at the beginning of my second term in the legislature, the caucus was influential enough to get a black man, Leroy Cain, elected assistant sergeant at arms for the S.C. House of Representatives. Cain had served as chauffeur to at least two South Carolina governors and was an asset to the people of the state. We were fortunate to have him in that newly created position. In addition the Legislative Black Caucus was influential in getting the first black State House tour guide, Andrena Davis, hired. She represented South Carolina so well during her years of service that people who were visiting from out of state more than twenty-five years ago still inquire for her!

Having black members in the legislature also resulted in certain laws, such as one dealing with discrimination where state funds were in use. In

1977, with a push from the Legislative Black Caucus, a law was enacted prohibiting the use of state funds to sponsor or defray the cost of any function by a state agency or institution at a club or organization that did not admit as members persons of all races, religions, colors, sexes, and national origins. A situation in Orangeburg relating to this law demonstrated that caucus members supported each other on issues that might come from another member's district.

In 1979 I made a request to the presidents of Clemson University and the University of South Carolina that they withdraw their golf teams from a tournament being played at the Country Club of Orangeburg. At that time the country club had no black members, and some white members had been told that any black guests of members would be unwelcome and asked to leave. Under these circumstances I didn't think it was appropriate or legal for these state-funded university teams to participate in a tournament there. Clemson University president Robert C. Edwards immediately withdrew the Clemson team, indicating that he understood and acknowledged the law. However, University of South Carolina president Dr. James B. Holderman decided that USC's team would go ahead and participate in the tournament.

When it became necessary to bring this situation to the attention of the public, the Black Legislative Caucus held a news conference at the State House. Of course by this time, the Country Club of Orangeburg had said that it would not bar any spectators from watching the tournament and that it was acceptable for the qualifying schools to bring black coaches or players. A day or so after the caucus's news conference exposing the situation, the University of South Carolina withdrew its team. A lone black representative could not have accomplished this without support from peers. As for the Country Club of Orangeburg, which has always been an attractive piece of real estate, many interracial functions are now held there, and I understand they have black members.

I served with some outstanding representatives in the Legislative Black Caucus. One of the most distinguished was Ernest Finney Jr., a lawyer from Sumter. He later became a South Carolina Supreme Court justice and several years ago retired as the state's first black chief justice. Hudson Barksdale, an educator from Spartanburg, distinguished himself by his dedication to representing his district. Kay Patterson, a former teacher from Columbia with whom I served, is still in the South Carolina legislature, now serving in the S.C. Senate. Sam Foster from Rock Hill was also impressive with his sincerity in serving his constituents. Among the ladies of the Legislative Black Caucus during my tenure, first Juanita Goggins from Rock Hill and later Juanita White from Hardeeville were effective in seeing issues from a female point of reference. I remember too that for a portion of the ten years I was a member, Robert Woods from Charleston served ably as chairman of the Legislative Black Caucus.

In addition to outstanding members, we had some aides who assisted us with caucus business and research. A few of these I remember are Jimmy Gilbert, Edward Francis, Robert Gist, John Gadsen, and Dalton Trezvant. All these gentlemen may not have worked exclusively for the caucus; some may have been from another office of state government. However, I do remember at one time or another they all added to what we were able to accomplish.

On June 9, 1979, the first annual South Carolina Legislative Black Caucus Dinner was held in Columbia. At that dinner we honored the black church. South Carolina governor Richard W. Riley spoke, as did the Honorable Louis Martin, special assistant to the president of the United States of America.

The Legislative Black Caucus added a voice in South Carolina that had been silent for nearly a hundred years. This situation paralleled that of other southern states during this period in our nation's history. The percentage of people in the black population in this state has historically been significantly higher than the percentage of blacks holding elective and appointed offices. Some things are a long time dawning on people to the point that they take action to bring about change, such as the fact that the House of *Representatives* is supposed to be just that—*representative* of the state's population. Blacks serving in the legislature could see things that whites overlooked or were not aware of.

Government Primer

It seems to me that at every level of government—whether municipal, county, state, or federal—one of the most important jobs an elected official has is to help citizens deal with the bureaucracy. It is only natural in employment situations, whether private or government, that employees respond to the goals laid out by those who sign their paychecks and/or have direct authority over the jobs they hold. For example, if one is employed at a county courthouse and has a supervisor who can promote, fire, or demote him, and increase or decrease his wages, that's who he pays attention to. So then let's say that ordinary Joe Citizen calls to get information and that employee is otherwise occupied and puts off Joe Citizen or promises to call him back and doesn't. Joe Citizen is not in a position to get that government employee to perform. However, if Joe Citizen calls his elected county official and outlines the struggle he's having getting service and if that official contacts the supervisor of the employee, then Joe Citizen has a better chance of getting the service that the county employee was hired to perform. When I served in the state legislature I found that contacting a department head in state government usually brought quick action.

The two most frequent requests I had from citizens during my ten years in the legislature were for help getting a job and getting roads paved. For the taxes citizens pay they are entitled to some services from government. Paved roads, to a certain extent, are among these services, and in our county it was one of the most difficult items for which to find adequate funding. The job requests were always a dilemma for me as an elected official. When I knew of any available jobs, I was always glad to put a constituent in touch with the proper authority. However, these jobs were few and far between despite the ever increasing governmental payrolls.

There were some jobs in the S.C. House and Senate for university students working as pages. As I recall, by the time I retired, each legislator was allotted one page. However, the longer a representative or senator was in office the more that person could learn about the existence of page positions in other State House locations. For instance, the lieutenant governor had several pages on staff; even though I had no jurisdiction there I could recommend and perhaps be successful in getting a constituent placed.

Pages are responsible for work that helps the legislative bodies function more smoothly. For example, when I served in the House, the pages were responsible for seeing that copies of proposed bills were put on each member's desk each day. Now, I imagine, this is done through computers. Delivering telephone messages to members during the sessions was a critical job because staying in touch with constituents was and is the number one priority of most elected officials. Pages' responsibilities also included distributing mail to members, clipping statewide newspaper articles about members, and helping the sergeant at arms control the main door leading into the House and Senate chambers. Some of these duties have shifted and changed from year to year, but they have always involved trying to aid the process of the state's business.

The students fortunate enough to get jobs as pages are subject to strict rules and a dress code. They are not allowed to read, study, or attend to personal affairs while they are on duty at the State House. Since the value of a page is increased by knowing the names of all the members, each page is given thirty days to learn them. In addition to having employment in a location close to their campus, pages are paid excellent wages and work in a desirable environment. They learn discipline and something about how government functions. Having a page position is similar to being awarded a scholarship in return for attending about fifteen or twenty hours of classes a week, the classroom being the State House. With the advent of the S.C. Legislative Black Caucus black college students, for the first time in any numbers, were also chosen for these positions.

Frequently visitors to sessions of the House and Senate at the State House come away with the impression that there is disorder in the proceedings. Senators and representatives are often not listening to other members when they are at the podium speaking. To observers in the overhead galleries, that is rude and disrespectful. Maybe so. But there is another way of seeing it. Most members know where they stand on a bill that is being presented or debated on the floor. We've gotten our "instructions" from our constituents because the bill has probably had a hearing before a committee or subcommittee and been publicized previously. By the time the bill makes it to consideration by the whole House or Senate, most members know how they will vote. Even so, the primary sponsors and opponents of the bills must be allowed to have their say because this is how our process of government works. As far as I can tell, no superior form of government has ever existed. It's one of those situations where perception and reality are vastly different matters.

A huge part of ensuring the survival of our republican form of government is to keep the operations of government out in the open. Even when this is done, it seems that some of the worst dangers existing in government are "hidden in plain sight" because people aren't paying attention. One of the most flagrant examples I saw during my terms in the legislature was the way state circuit judges were voted on by lawyer-legislators. Historically it's been natural for lawyers to offer for public office and consequently to be elected. After all, they've studied laws; why shouldn't they make them? In my estimation their percentages in legislative bodies in this country have historically been too high because many exert a strong-arm influence when recommending laws that in effect protect the legal profession and ensure clients.

Circuit judges come before the legislature in South Carolina for election, and many come up for reelection every ten years. The same lawyer-legislators voting on these judges also try cases before them. Common sense tells me this shouldn't be. As you read this, maybe you're thinking,

"Well, Middleton, you were there for ten years. Why didn't you get a law passed to change it?" The answer lies in the high percentage of those in the legal profession who continue to be elected and perpetuate these systems.

Of course, in order to get things accomplished for citizens, elected officials have to have competent assistance. Standing committees in the S.C. House and Senate each had at least a couple of staff members when I served; maybe there are more for each committee now. The Labor, Commerce and Industry Committee on which I served had two outstanding employees, I remember. Dottie Nidiffer was the administrative assistant, and Michael Moloney, a young attorney from Charleston, was our staff counsel. Anyone who's served in elective office or dealt much with elected governmental officials knows that competent staff members are the ones who get the work done. The elected official is in such demand for attendance at public functions that staff is absolutely vital. In addition to whatever staff were provided in state positions, some elected officials, including me, paid for extra help out of our legislative salaries.

Along with the work in the legislature came some rewards of recognition. In 1979 I was honored by the Boy Scouts of America with the Silver Beaver Award. The Indian Waters Council here in South Carolina nominated me to receive the highest award given in Scouting for the years I had served as scoutmaster and for the subsequent financial support I had given the organization. It gave me a lot of satisfaction to know that during my years as leader our troop at Trinity United Methodist Church had produced the first black to earn the rank of Eagle Scout in the Indian Waters Council.

I saw service on the Governor's Committee for the Employment of the Handicapped while I was in the legislature. In addition, I was selected as a member of the Board of Visitors at Clemson University. Somehow during this time period, I also managed to give service on the board of the Methodist Home (now the Oaks) in Orangeburg.

Reapportionment and Senate Campaign

After I had served more than nine years in the S.C. House of Representatives, a lot of citizens in Orangeburg County let me know that they thought, because I was open to and approachable by so many different kinds of people, I could better serve them in the S.C. Senate. They knew that they could reach me at home by phone at night, if need be, to help them with their needs, and they felt that such accessibility was extraordinary for a public servant.

After this urging by many people, both black and white, in Orangeburg County, I agreed to offer for the S.C. Senate. Actually, I think by this time a small portion of Barnwell County was also included in that district. The time had come after five successful terms in the S.C. House of Representatives to see if the people were willing to elect me to the Senate. If not, I felt that five terms were enough for one person. I had my own internal clock about "term limits," which are much under discussion today.

My staff and I knew that mounting a campaign for the S.C. Senate was not going to be an easy job. For starters, the House and Senate districts in South Carolina had to be redrawn by those bodies before elections were held. As was usual with the tough decisions, members of the legislature put off this vital business until the eleventh hour. Everyone knew that to avoid legal hassles with the U.S. Justice Department there had to be a certain number of majority black districts drawn in each representative body.

The de facto difficulty in reapportioning the state House and Senate is that some current members are always going to have some of the area containing their strongest election supporters drawn out of their present district and put into another. Some senators and representatives have enough clout with other members of the legislature that their districts are protected during the process, and thus they are ensured of reelection. In 1984 this was the case with Orangeburg state senator Marshall B. Williams.

Williams, an attorney and World War II navy veteran, had served for thirty-two years in the S.C. Senate. He resided in his plantation-style home on the eastern outskirts of the city of Orangeburg, a location that could be placed in either of the two largely Orangeburg County Senate districts that would continue to exist after reapportionment. It was a virtual certainty that a member of the Legislative Black Caucus from Orangeburg County, John Matthews, would also run for the S.C. Senate.

Of course, the Senate district to be drawn for Williams would be a white majority district, and the adjoining district would be a black majority district. As much as voters *say* they are against districts that are decided by racial percentages, rarely do they back up this rhetoric at the ballot boxes. Historically in this state and in this country, whites elect whites, and blacks elect blacks. There are prominent exceptions in some areas of the country, such as former U.S. congressman J. C. Watts of Oklahoma and former Virginia governor Douglas Wilder, but usually the electorate votes for members of their own race. This is especially true in the South. Racial percentages were vital.

I had already announced I would run for the Senate without knowing where the lines would be drawn. It was well known that during my tenure in the House I had served my constituents with extraordinary attention to keeping people informed about what was transpiring in state government. I had participated in local occasions regularly, made decisions fairly without regard to skin color, and endeavored to conduct myself with dignity.

It was also well known that I was an independent thinker in representing the wishes of the voters in House District 95. Members of the legislative power structure knew that Earl Middleton was strong in staying true to the wishes of his district and would not "go along to get along" as would a person with weaker resolve. Although they knew I would do the right thing, they also knew I could not be "handled" according to their wishes. I would not cave in to satisfy their goals.

These characteristics were representative too of a large core of the voters in House District 95, which included highly educated blacks working as professors and administrators at Claflin and S.C. State, as well as many educated upper- and upper-middle-class whites. At election time politicians were frightened to death of independent-thinking, educated voters. During reapportionment the two areas that were considered the least desirable to have in one's district in Orangeburg were the Country Club of Orangeburg area and the Parlerdale area. Educated whites largely composed the former, and highly educated blacks composed the latter. They were considered the least desirable by most politicians because they were the best informed and could not be led en masse by an election boss to go for a certain candidate.

Because I represented this group and had these same independent decision-making characteristics, the good-ole-boy network at the S.C. State House knew they could not count on Earl Middleton to do their bidding. As a result they drew the Senate lines so that Senator Williams and I would be running in the same district. I distinctly remember Speaker of the House Robert Sheheen, from Camden, coming by my desk to let me know this had been decided. That was fine with me, although at the same time the legislative power brokers figured they had "sold Middleton down the river," to borrow a phrase from slave times.

Because of the reputation I had crafted during my ten years in the House I was confident that I could get a large enough percentage of the white voters and black voters combined to be elected. The census figures used to determine district lines showed about 50 to 51 percent whites in the District 40 S.C. Senate area in 1980. However, the effective percentage was closer to 56 percent white because students at Claflin and S.C. State, while counted in the census and reapportionment figures used to carve out districts, were for the most part required to vote in their hometown precincts and not in Orangeburg. Washington was too far away for the U.S. Justice Department to understand how the good ole boys in the state legislature were superior in their remap math.

My staff and I were not concerned about all these shenanigans among South Carolina's entrenched power players. We planned to run a campaign staffed by volunteers. To give some professional direction to our efforts, we employed a campaign consultant from adjoining Lexington County, Rod Shealy. A veteran of many campaigns, Rod had worked with Democratic candidates, and he had worked with Republican candidates. We set up a campaign strategy based on contacting voters directly. Fred Broughton, a black Orangeburg businessman, graciously consented to become manager of the campaign.

This contest immediately became high profile because it was the first time in thirty-two years that Senator Williams had an opponent in "his" senate district. It is an axiom in the American political arena that after a person has been in office a long time, that office is seen as belonging to him or her. This view is commonly taken not only by the occupant but also by people in general. This perception is dangerous. People should remember that in reality every elective office in this country belongs to those voting in the elections.

With a large cadre of volunteers, we went to work. Our campaign headquarters was set up in a large house I had recently purchased on Russell Street near S.C. State University. In previous years it had been home to the Wallace Bethea family. Bethea had owned J. W. Smoak Hardware, was an official at Orangeburg's First National Bank, and had served on the S.C. State University Board of Trustees. We knew we didn't have the money to outspend the Williams campaign, but we knew we could outwork it. Our volunteers were dedicated. They put in many hours, and our headquarters was humming with activity from early in the morning until late in the evening most nights.

Early in the campaign Williams apparently suffered a slight stroke and had to curtail his personal activities. My sense of ethics led me to handle this development with more reticence than I would ordinarily have used in a closely contested political campaign. This is where his superior campaign treasury gave him the advantage. His camp saw to it that the district was plastered with signs. There were campaign flyers and billboards everywhere. Plenty of print and media ads also blanketed the district. Even so we had a good plan and stuck to it, consistently continuing to contact voters. After a while Williams declared that he had recovered from his illness. By this time he knew he had the fight of his political life on his hands.

The October 2, 1984, election was actually the Democratic primary, which had been delayed because of the holdup in Senate reapportionment. We knew that many of Williams's supporters had voted in the Republican primary the previous June. Under state law a person was entitled to vote in only one primary for that office per election. Therefore, those who had voted in the Republican primary should not have been entitled to vote again in the Democratic primary. We had poll watchers at each precinct with a list of those who had already voted in the Republican primary. Our poll watchers challenged the votes of those persons after they had revoted. Of course, those voters who had their second votes challenged were not happy about it, but the law is the law. Or it should have been. This time South Carolina attorney general Travis Medlock decided these people could vote twice!

When all was said and done, the Williams camp managed to have a little over a thousand votes more in their column than our side had in ours. The challenged votes came to about four hundred, not enough to have changed the outcome.

On election night our supporters gathered at our Russell Street headquarters to await the vote count. As soon as we knew for sure that Williams had more votes, Bernice and I went to Williams's law office and congratulated him and his wife. Still today I hear about supposed voting irregularities that are alleged to have occurred, allowing Williams to win. But I've forgotten about the personal effects of that election years ago.

Several days following the election we went to a hearing concerning the challenged ballots and formally dropped our challenges. In my opinion the people had spoken. In accordance with the oath I had taken to support the nominee of the Democratic Party, I voted for Williams in the November general election. He returned to the S.C. Senate and served until his death.

Senator Williams and I never had any problems after that election. We've done business with his law firm in the years since and still do. Following Senator Williams's death in late 1995, his son Charles complimented his father and me for not becoming bitter rivals after our contest for the same S.C. Senate seat. Marshall Williams and I both understood that the office belonged to the people, not to either of us.

Legislative Legacy

Within the past five years I have learned that one hundred years before I was elected to the South Carolina General Assembly in 1974 my grand-uncle Benjamin W. Middleton served in that body from 1872 to 1874. He was my granddaddy Abram's brother and represented Barnwell County from Midway, South Carolina, which is now part of Bamberg County and adjoins Orangeburg to the south.

Part Four

Enduring

8

Business in the Next Generation

After our son, Kenny, graduated from Furman University in 1977, he decided he would like to work in our family's real estate and insurance business. I had not pushed him in that direction. However, he was well prepared, having earned a degree in business.

After being in the business for twenty years, Kenny explained in an interview why he decided to come to work with me:

> I think although Dad wanted me to be a part of what he had built, he did not use the strategy of pushing it down my throat, which was probably a good decision. I was able to see him work and I was able to see the things he was able to accomplish. I did see that he had to work very hard to make the strides he made. But we felt like we were prepared for that. I was an athlete in high school and college; so I was not a stranger to hard work.
>
> Coming back to Orangeburg to live and work in the business was not an easy decision. I was prepared by college to work for companies such as Xerox and IBM, where I did have offers. Then I thought that if I was going to use whatever talents I had to make a company more successful that I should, at least, come back home and attempt to build on what he had spent his lifetime building. My curiosity was to see what I could do with the education they had provided me by putting it to the test here in the home town business.
>
> During the summers I had worked in the business doing carpentry, painting and other manual labor in an attempt to learn from the bottom up. Dad taught me about investing in real estate and at a very

young age I was able to do some of that and make many of the property repairs myself. He is one that allows you to learn and make your own mistakes. He will allow you to grow and I think you become a better person having these experiences.

So he did not really sit me down and say, "I want you to come back; I want you to come home." But when I told him, I could tell he was very happy that decision had been made.

He allows me, at the present time, to run the company most any way I see fit, overlooking things in a very quiet manner. But at the same time he's making sure we don't make too many mistakes and that we're headed in the direction he thinks is appropriate for the operation in the long run. So, it's been a pleasure.

When Kenny came on board our business began to grow significantly. He wasn't exaggerating when he said he could work hard. Watching his enthusiasm and dedicated work gave me a fresh incentive about the business. Some of the decisions I had made in previous years also began to pay off. For example, joining the National Association of Realtors and corresponding state and local organizations put us in touch with a group of professionals across the country from whose expertise we could benefit.

Never will I forget the generosity of a fellow Realtor from Denver, Colorado, William M. Moore. Moore was the owner of a multioffice real estate company in that state. He had many years of experience as a broker-owner and ran very successful offices. His agents were top-notch, and he knew how to train them to rise to their highest potential through outstanding client service. He was expert in business organization and time management.

At some point, several years after Kenny had come into our business, Moore was scheduled to be in Columbia in connection with his duties as an official with the National Association of Realtors. We wrote to Moore ahead of time and requested a private session with him in Columbia to advise us on brokerage management. We knew we needed help, but because real estate brokerage is very competitive at the local level, we needed someone from out of state. Moore spent an entire morning meeting with Kenny, Joy, and me about proper company organization. In addition to Moore's generosity with his time, he was an extremely considerate gentleman. It was easy to see why he was successful in a business that largely involves dealing with people. It was no surprise to us several years later when Moore was elected president of the National Association of Realtors for 1987.

Ralph Roberts is a Realtor in Detroit, Michigan, who has been one of the top-selling agents in the country. Some years Ralph sells upward of four hundred homes. Obviously he has a well-organized business plan and knows how to get along with people in order to accomplish this feat of closing, on average, more than one property a day. Some years back Roberts traveled to Orangeburg and spoke to our company's agents at the annual awards banquet.

Another top Realtor who has been generous and kind with her help to us is Joan Pate of Salt Lake City, Utah. For several decades Joan has been one of the most consistent and top-selling agents in the country. She earns more selling real estate than brain surgeons do performing surgery. Joan has traveled to Orangeburg on more than one occasion to guide our agents in their business planning and to conduct workshops. Moore, Roberts, and Pate are outstanding examples of the generous and helpful people we've met through contacts in Realtor organizations.

By the time I completed my legislative service in 1984, our real estate brokerage business had taken tremendous leaps forward in the Orangeburg marketplace. That's the area of the company Kenny heads up. It was about this time that we worked with an out-of-town real estate investor who was interested in building some condominiums near the colleges at the corner of Russell and Clarendon streets. Joy Barnes was successful in finding a suitable piece of land. After a lot of work and negotiation, we arrived at an agreeable price, and the land transaction was consummated. Subsequently a twenty-eight-unit complex was constructed and named Clarendon Place. It became the first condominium project in Orangeburg, and the units are still in use.

In 1985 the Coldwell Banker real estate franchise, which was then owned by Sears and Roebuck, decided that the Orangeburg residential real estate market was large enough that it would be worth their while to affiliate with a local broker. They sent in their market analysts to figure out which companies were brokering what amounts of business and with whom. They interviewed bankers, attorneys, appraisers, Realtor executives, and real estate brokers and agents, as well as scouring the courthouse records for property transactions.

We had considered a franchise affiliation for our company before but had decided against it because we didn't think that particular connection would help us with our clients. However, Coldwell Banker operated on a higher plane. Seeking to be connected with a firm that was at the top of the market in every regard, they were looking for a company that had a large market share and owners with integrity. They knew from a business viewpoint that the franchise owners' integrity was insurance against future problems and unnecessary friction.

An investigation by the Coldwell Banker Residential Affiliates revealed that the Middleton Agency had the largest market share of any real estate company in Orangeburg. We were surprised and happy. We knew that we had worked diligently in all areas of the community. We had black agents, and we had white agents, about half and half. And that's about where our market was—about half our clients and customers were black and about half were white. We had been so busy working that we had never stopped to count our market share. Officials of Coldwell Banker Residential Affiliates invited us to a meeting in Atlanta at their southeastern regional headquarters to discuss a franchise. Kenny and I agreed to go and asked Joy Barnes to accompany us.

We saw that there would be business advantages to having our name connected with a respected national real estate franchise. It would be worth the enormous amounts we were required to remit to be in a position to add more value for our clients. These were the kinds of factors that weighed on our decision to affiliate with Coldwell Banker. At the time this advancement for our company was as positive as that of signing on Joy and George Barnes as agents in 1972.

As a part of our initial relationship with Coldwell Banker Residential Affiliates it was necessary for us to travel to southern California, the location of their national headquarters. California has historically been on the leading edge of advancement in real estate brokerage, and Colbert Coldwell and Benjamin Banker began their company in San Francisco following that city's great earthquake in the early 1900s. It is thus apparent that the name of our affiliate has nothing to do with the banking business but rather is the surname of a company founder.

In southern California we met with the president of Coldwell Banker Residential Affiliates and other company officers, and we learned their organizational and affiliate procedures. We spent time in real estate brokerage offices with the latest equipment set up so that individual agents could perform with maximum efficiency in client service. After getting a full overview of the operation we made the mutual decision to become a Coldwell Banker Residential Affiliate. Of course, at the same time we were making up our minds the Coldwell Banker officials were looking us over too because each company is independently owned. They wanted affiliates who would represent their name in local communities throughout the country with quality service, sincerity, and integrity.

After doing our investigations and considering all the factors involved, we officially and mutually agreed on our "business marriage." We became the first black-owned company in the country to become affiliated with Coldwell Banker. I was glad that Kenny could have the advantages associated with a national real estate powerhouse as he continued to build the brokerage business. Our contract of affiliation with the national Coldwell Banker Residential Affiliates continues to this day, having been renewed several times.

This move was the impetus for many positive things Kenny has implemented since he has been managing the real estate brokerage part of our business. For example, Kenny has been a leader in our marketplace in raising the level of client service by implementing a new pattern for agent recognition. Many years ago he began an Agent of the Month recognition program that feeds into an Agent of the Year award given annually at our agent-employee banquet. One method he uses to almost ensure that our agents are the best educated in the marketplace is a concept he calls "Convention Bucks." Each month he awards to the top three or four agents, according to sales, dollar credits that can be used to attend real estate education sessions. Because real estate agents pay their own expenses this amounts to more money to them.

Most real estate companies have weekly sales meetings. Kenny goes a step beyond and expands each of his meetings to include mini education sessions for our agents. He has a written agenda outlining each meeting. This may sound basic, but—from what I've been told—in real estate brokerage companies it is not usually done. In addition to many other improvements, too numerous to mention, inside our company, Kenny has also been a leader in the Realtor organization. He has served two terms as president of the local board, and his opinion is sought after at the state level.

One of the reasons that we have been successful carrying our business into the second generation is that Kenny has excellent people skills, honed by his education at Furman University. Even though he was in the extreme minority when he graduated in 1977, the experience of being in that situation gives him the ability to deal with anyone he encounters in the business world. (I think fewer than 5 percent of his fellow graduates were black.) This type of benefit should be a consideration for every family of African descent as they select colleges or universities for their children. Although our historically black colleges and universities are still doing a Herculean job of educating students who attend them, the choice of an educational facility should be weighed with an open mind. The main thing is knowing who you (or your children) are and what area needs to be strengthened educationally. In Kenny's case he understood that and is now serving on the board of trustees at Claflin University, where our family has so much history.

In addition Kenny prepared himself to succeed in the real estate business by taking a series of courses offered through the Realtor groups. These courses led to his earning three professional real estate designations: GRI (Graduate Realtor Institute), CRS (Certified Residential Specialist), and CRB (Certified Real Estate Brokerage Manager). He also influenced other agents in our company to do likewise.

Black Folks Gotta Learn

In connection with discussing our real estate and insurance business going into the next generation, I want to expand these thoughts to the position in which we as black people find ourselves in these times. Just as Kenny has changed methods that we implement for moving our business forward, blacks must change the way we think about moving our lives ahead. We can no longer, as a group, expect to make progress by using outdated techniques and strategies. For example, in the early 1960s many blacks were denied the right to vote. To protest this injustice blacks (including myself) marched en mass in protest in public places on a regular basis. These ongoing mass demonstrations created an awareness of the unfairness being perpetrated on a group because of race and skin color. As a result Congress passed laws and created enforcement mechanisms to correct this situation for the most part. Blacks now have essentially full access at the voting booth as a way to speak to lawmakers and those in authority. This is now one of the techniques we should be using to improve our lives. Street demonstrations are outmoded as a way of accomplishing goals in this country. Every great now and then a demonstration can be a way to make a statement, but the supposed black leaders who are still trying to revive mass protests need to update their thinking.

Education must continue to be in the forefront as a "way out" of poverty and poor health habits, which continue to plague blacks. Education includes far more than simply going through school. Education means reading newspapers and books every day. Education means being around people who are not like you. Education means traveling. Education means exhibiting common sense. Education means exposing yourself to new ideas. Education means taking care of your health with adequate rest, regular physical exercise, and proper nutrition. Education means learning to exercise good judgment about the way you live your life. Education means living on less money than you make and saving the remainder. Education means enrolling at the very best schools possible. Education means expanding your thinking.

As a group we have made much progress, for which we can be proud. We should celebrate our accomplishments. These often come one person at a time. An outstanding example that has touched my life is that of a young black gentleman from "not one of the best neighborhoods" in Orangeburg who was being raised by his grandparents. In the spring of 1994, as a high school senior, Jaime Harrison appeared at our weekly Kiwanis Club meeting in connection with the fact that he had been awarded a scholarship to Yale University. That this young black man had won a scholarship to Yale was especially impressive to me because I knew he had to overcome steep financial and social odds to achieve this. As we left the meeting, I congratulated Jaime and offered to help him any way I could. About a week later he came to my office and told me he was required to have a laptop computer when he enrolled at Yale the coming fall. I agreed to let him assist at my office to earn the money he needed for his laptop. That was a win-win situation for both of us.

Jaime was very successful at Yale. In his junior year he was elected class treasurer, and for two years he was president of Pierson Residential College. He earned his undergraduate degree from Yale and his law degree from Georgetown University School of Law in Washington, D.C., and he began working on the staff of Congressman James Clyburn. Jaime served as executive director of the House Democratic Caucus while Clyburn was chairman. In January 2007, when the Democratic majority took over the leadership positions in Congress, Clyburn became the House majority whip. Jaime then became director of floor operations and counsel, the first black person ever to hold this position in the U.S. House of Representatives.

In using Jaime Harrison as an example of how a black person can succeed, I've also touched on Congressman James Clyburn's success as a black man. While his biography would make another book, I will say that through his influence one of the Democratic presidential debates was broadcast live from Orangeburg, South Carolina, on nationwide television in April 2007 during the 2008 presidential election campaign.

At the same time we celebrate accomplishments, we need to continue our progress. Blacks need to be more mindful of building a net financial worth beyond what it will take to pay next month's credit card minimums.

It is absolutely imperative for us to find a way to keep our young men from being incarcerated in record numbers. We've got to lower the high percentage of babies being born outside marriage; men and women are equally responsible in these situations. How can we expect to keep our people out of prisons if they are born without the benefit of two parents on the scene? We no longer have the excuse of being raped by the slave master; we are doing it to ourselves.

We can't afford to think of education just as "getting through school." We must consider it as something we do for our entire lives. During my work years I labored at many different endeavors, including agricultural, shoe making, cooking, carpentry, postal service, and barbering, before finally settling on insurance and real estate. This was before the advent of the personal computer with all its technological possibilities. Reeducating ourselves and continuing to educate ourselves are musts in this world. We are already in a time when the average worker will change *professions* (not just jobs) several times during her or his career. The only way to prepare for this successfully is with constant self-education.

It is even possible, I found, to add education in your life while serving others. In 1988 I was asked by members of the state legislature to serve on the South Carolina Supreme Court's Board of Commissioners on Grievance and Discipline. The majority of the dozen or so members were, of course, lawyers, but the legislature had mandated that two members be from the public at large. We met approximately once a month and considered complaints that had been lodged against attorneys. After considering the severity of the charges, we made recommendations to the members of the S.C. Supreme Court as to what actions, if any, we felt should be taken. More often than not the complaints filed involved mishandling clients' money. There was a lot of common sense involved in this work, and we had to be very objective. An even, judicial temperament was a must for board members. Serving in this capacity for six years until 1994 taught me even more about the way the legal profession works than I had learned during my years in the S.C. General Assembly. As with every profession, I found that a large dose of integrity and hard work was the best way to advance.

Wall Street Journal Story

April 29, 1992, was a defining moment in the history of our business at the Middleton companies. That day's edition of the *Wall Street Journal* carried an extremely positive front-page story on our businesses with a picture of me above the centerfold. It was one of those days for which a person works a lifetime, and it is an achievement that was made possible by the work of many others around me.

Since its inception in 1889 the *Wall Street Journal* has been one of the most respected national business publications in America. It covers all aspects of business with stories, images, charts, graphs, statistics, and more. There are several international editions, and the publication is printed and distributed from several areas within this country. Most important, it is published each business day. To sum it up in language that the ordinary person can readily understand, I'll paraphrase one of my Middleton in-laws, who said to me shortly after our article appeared, "The *Wall Street Journal* is the white people's bible." I'll go further and say that it's probably the businessperson's bible.

That story was a BIG DEAL to us and still is. We are still getting positive feedback as a result of that story fifteen years ago. Many people have asked us how it came about. Here's the story.

For many years Joy Barnes had been a regular *Wall Street Journal* reader. She told me that when she did consulting work for the South Carolina Electric and Gas Company Shareholders' Association it was required reading. Paul Quattlebaum, who headed up the association at that time, made a subscription to the publication a part of Joy's compensation package. I do know, for a fact, that she read it each day.

In addition to enhancing her capabilities with the SCANA group (which is the name of the company SCE&G evolved into), Joy also brought many items of interest to the attention of our small business. For example, one evening in 1983 about 10:00 P.M. Joy phoned me at home to say there was a book review titled "Charleston on Her Mind" in the *Wall Street Journal* that seemed to involve my ancestors. She said the names Abram Middleton and J. B. Middleton had jumped off the page as she read because she had heard me talk so much of my granddaddy through the years. It so happened that this was a review of *Lemon Swamp and Other Places: A Carolina Memoir,* which had recently been written by Mamie Garvin Fields, my cousin, and her granddaughter Karen Fields. At another time Joy noticed in a 1991 issue of the *Wall Street Journal* that there was to be an upcoming issue on black entrepreneurship. Immediately, she said, the wheels in her brain began to turn.

Joy had been our top real estate salesperson for years, accomplishing that by independently educating herself on the subject. She spent a phenomenal amount of her time and income attending specialized courses so she could do a better job handling business for her clients and customers. One phase of her training involved "cold calling." She would get on the phone and ask anyone in Orangeburg, "When are you planning on moving?" We are, after all is said and done, in the "asking business."

When Joy learned that there would be a special edition of the *Wall Street Journal* on black businesses she knew instinctively that our business was unusual enough to be represented with a story. The next day she used these cold-calling techniques and phoned the main switchboard at the newspaper's office in New York City. She asked to speak with the editor who would be handling that particular upcoming issue and was connected to Roger Ricklefs. In fewer than sixty seconds she told him the bare-bones story of our company. He gave her the answer she had expected by saying that all the stories for that issue had been decided on and written already.

Joy could not believe what she was hearing next when Ricklefs added, "But I want to do a story on your company for another issue." He went on to tell her that he would have a reporter contact her within the next week to get going on the story. Joy said that he was very definite with this immediate decision. I think possibly she called him back once before being contacted by the reporter assigned to do the story, Dorothy J. Gaiter.

As soon as she contacted Joy, Dorothy began her work from New York by telephone, interviewing people and collecting information. She had asked for a list of people to talk with about us, and apparently she worked for two weeks from her New York office before she traveled to Orangeburg. On her arrival in Orangeburg for a week's work, we knew immediately that this was going to be a learning experience for us in how a top-notch national newspaper gets the job done. Dorothy immediately began interviewing not only people we had on the list but also some others we knew were not favorably inclined toward me politically. We learned that this was a specific portion of her assignment and is the way a good reporter works, by interviewing those with varying opinions.

We found that a good reporter checks each bit of information for accuracy and verifies everything. As the week progressed we grew fond of Dorothy and saw that she was able to relate to everyone she met and interviewed. At the same time she was very professional in the way she worked, not spending too much time or becoming too involved with any one person. She was constantly in touch by phone with her editor at the *Wall Street Journal* office in New York. She was literally all over town talking to people, checking clip files at the *Times and Democrat* office, and doing research at the local library. Also she read as much about Orangeburg as possible.

Dorothy is a petite black woman, and she had a short Afro hairstyle. At some point during the week she showed us a photo of her two young daughters. Their skin was much lighter than Dorothy's. When we remarked on that she showed us a photo of her white husband. We really knew then that the publication couldn't have selected a better individual to report our story.

At some point during the construction of the article we were told by a *Wall Street Journal* official that many successful businesspeople come to their attention seeking articles. That official explained that our business was chosen because of the rarity of a black-owned business that had blacks and whites working with a racially mixed clientele. Also they liked stories that had not already appeared in other national publications. We were amazed to learn that our business was unique in this regard. As far as we had known, there were other businesses that mirrored ours over the country.

We didn't know how the story would come out, but we knew the *Wall Street Journal* was serious about running it. Dorothy's editor told her our story had been chosen for a page-one feature. Bernice and I spent many hours with Dorothy at our home and showing her our lake house. After she returned to New York, she worked another week on the story to finish it. At that point we nervously awaited publication of the article. I believe I remember being notified by Dorothy the afternoon before publication, which gave us time to reach the *Wall Street Journal*'s Charlotte, North Carolina, printing facility to arrange for delivery of extra copies.

The day the article appeared the reaction was immediate and positive. (See Appendix 3.) Our phones began to ring with calls from all over the country. The callers included friends as well as many we didn't know. We appreciated every one. We are to this day still getting positive ripples from that story, and we have stayed in touch with Dorothy Gaiter. She and her husband still write for the *Wall Street Journal*. In fact, they now create a weekly wine column for the weekend section of the journal and have published books on their experiences with wine.

Bernice

Each year for about fifteen years the BellSouth phone company has chosen to publish an African American history calendar as one of its corporate projects. Each month they feature the biography of a black South

Carolinian. The calendars are used primarily in schools to spotlight African American history all year. In 1995 I was chosen as one of the subjects for the upcoming 1996 edition of the calendar.

In connection with the calendar each year a big celebration and ceremony is held in October at the Koger Center in Columbia. It is one of the best-organized events with which I've been involved. Each honoree is asked to invite a dozen or so special guests to share the evening. Usually a couple of the honorees are deceased, in which case their descendants accept their awards and celebrate their success. BellSouth presents each honoree with a large framed drawing of his or her likeness as it appears on the calendar. The calendars are distributed immediately following the formal ceremony. Then there is a gigantic dessert buffet reception, and honorees are usually asked by many to sign their calendars. It is truly a first-class event.

Bernice had been having trouble with circulation in her legs and feet for several years. Walking more than a few steps was a problem for her by this time. There was a question as to whether or not her health would permit her to be with me that evening. She made the decision that we'd get a wheelchair for the evening, and she'd go. The evening was a huge success, and Bernice looked wonderful in her evening gown. All three of our children and their spouses were there, as I recall. My brothers Sam and Phillip, Phillip's wife, Vivian, and my sister Dorothy Louise Middleton also attended. What can be better for anyone than a celebration with his family and friends? I'll never forget that night.

For the first time that evening we met the owner of Middleton Place, a plantation in Charleston; Charles Duell and his son Holland were invited as special guests. BellSouth also presented a video on each honoree's life. The producers wanted to include a film clip from Middleton Place in mine as that is where my great-grandfather is said to have been enslaved. Except for Christmas a couple of months later, that was our last significant celebration together as a complete family.

On January 3, 1996, I went home from the office around midday to check on Bernice. I told her I was going to the bank, and she asked me to deposit a check for her. When I inquired if she wanted some juice, she said she didn't. As she had been sick most of the night, her response didn't surprise me. Then she reconsidered and said she would like juice. As I turned to go get it, I heard her gasp, and, looking back, I saw that she was unconscious. As I tried to revive her, I also called 911.

The ambulance arrived, and the paramedics immediately began trying to revive her. "Has her heart stopped?" I asked an EMS worker. "Yes, but we're going to try to get it going again," she replied. I put in a call for Kenny to come, and, after he arrived, we followed the emergency vehicle to the Regional Medical Center (hospital). When we got to the emergency room entrance, the paramedics stayed in the vehicle with Bernice, continuing to try to resuscitate her. Finally she was taken inside, and for an hour or so we had some hope she'd pull through. But it was not to be.

That February would have marked fifty years of marriage for us. Bernice and I had known each other since childhood. We had been friends many years before we were sweethearts. Several days after her death we had her final service at Trinity United Methodist, where both of our families have so much history. That was the hardest day I've ever lived through in my life. Being forced to say good-bye to someone you've loved many years is always difficult. When that person is also the closest one in the world to you it is doubly so.

Not only was I proud of Bernice as a beautiful wife and a wonderful mother to our children, but also I felt the accomplishments she made in her profession were significant for a black woman of her time. Many of these achievements I have already mentioned, but there is one that I believe epitomizes her professional success.

In 1977 Alex Haley, the acclaimed author of *Roots,* spoke at South Carolina State. At this time a television miniseries of *Roots* had a highly publicized airing, which millions watched nationwide. It can arguably be said that *Roots* was the most important piece of black literature in the twentieth century. Alex Haley was the genius who had researched and labored for years getting this story of his family's history traced back to Africa. After his book was written and published, it became an instant best-seller.

To have this celebrity speaking to a group in Orangeburg was a milestone. When Haley spoke at State, Bernice was chosen to introduce him to the student body, her faculty colleagues, and guests. I do not know who chose her for this honor or why. Perhaps it was because she was chair of the Department of Library Science and so seemed to be the appropriate faculty member for the task. Her introduction of Haley was not only eloquent; it was also correctly done. Never did she mention him by name until the last sentence. Haley's visit was extremely well received and represented the talent that we have been able to attract to Orangeburg for more than a hundred years because of the existence of our two historically black colleges and universities. And was I ever proud of my wife!

The Invitation

In the spring of 1996 I received a call from Charles H. P. Duell, the proprietor of Middleton Place plantation, requesting a meeting with Kenny and me. Middleton Place is the ancestral home of Arthur Middleton, who was one of the fifty-six signers of America's Declaration of Independence in 1776. It is located on the outskirts of Charleston, South Carolina, about eighteen miles northwest of the city. The grounds at Middleton Place include what are known as the oldest landscaped gardens in America.

Unlike most other families whose ancestors owned large plantations before the Civil War, the Middleton descendants have managed to retain ownership of their historic property from before the Revolutionary War to the present day. Several generations back Middleton Place was inherited by a female family member, and this is the reason it's no longer owned by a person with the Middleton surname.

Duell, who is a direct descendant of Arthur Middleton, invited us to become involved with Middleton Place Foundation, which was formed in the 1970s to administer the house museum and approximately a hundred acres around it, including the gardens. He asked me to serve on the foundation's board of trustees, and, when I retired, he invited Kenny to succeed me.

Historically black folks and plantations have gone together like prisoners and jailhouses. When prisoners get out of jail, most don't want to return. This is the same feeling many blacks have about plantations; they want nothing to do with them. Black families have passed down to their children the picture of plantations as being places where blacks were kept enslaved, shackled in chains, beaten, and mistreated. Some of this is true for all slaves, and for some slaves all, unfortunately, was true.

In my own particular case our family had a good sense of who we were from day one. We knew we were descended from Methodist ministers and that Granddaddy Middleton had been well respected when he was living and had set the values by which our family lived. As I've mentioned before, my parents never discussed the racial situation directly with us and certainly never mentioned anything about slavery. Actually we never knew whether our ancestors had been enslaved or free. In my cousin Mamie's memoir, *Lemon Swamp*, she cites a servant-master relationship between our ancestors and the white Middletons. Knowing for sure that our family was from Charleston, many assumed, and still do, that our ancestors were from Middleton Place.

It is within this context that we heard Duell's invitation. As we learned, Duell is not a stereotypical descendant of a southern landowner. For starters he was born in New York City in 1938. He was educated at private northeastern schools before earning his degree from Yale and continuing with advanced education in France. He became a New York banker and worked at that profession for some years. More important to our connection, when he was a teenager, he began to come to Charleston in the summers to help his grandparents at Middleton Place. They were responsible for beginning the modern-day restoration of the historic gardens on the property.

Middleton Place was passed to Charles through his mother, who, unfortunately, had died at a young age. Shortly afterward, I believe in the 1970s, Charles and his wife moved their family of four young children into the house at Middleton Place. They resided there for some years before the rebuilt house was opened to the public for tours. In the years that Charles has owned and managed this historic property he has, in my opinion, been the absolute epitome of the good steward. As I understand it, when the property came to him through his mother and grandparents, who had brought it through the Great Depression and World War II, there was much work to be done and very little cash with which to do it. Thanks to Charles, Middleton Place has become a showplace of American history. It is in the same category of properties as the Virginia homes of George Washington at Mount Vernon and Thomas Jefferson at Monticello.

When Kenny and I received this invitation, I was intrigued with the possibility of service on the Middleton Place Foundation's board for several reasons, including the fact that I would become the first black person to be a member of this group, whose duty was primarily oversight. We were responsible for seeing that the financial aspects of the foundation were in order and being handled correctly.

While many blacks are put off by the thought of being on a plantation, my mind was working in another direction. Today's Middleton Place principals were there to preserve a historical property and interpret the lives of those who had lived and worked there. Whether it was positive or negative for my people, it was our history. That history is going to be told whether I or any other black person serves on the board. So if I am interested in having anything to say about it then it seemed to be a no-brainer to accept Charles's invitation and get involved.

As soon as I accepted membership on the board at Middleton Place I began to educate myself for the task. The timing was perfect as I learned of a symposium, "The Grand Estate—Yesterday, Today and Tomorrow," that was to be held in Charlottesville, Virginia, within the next sixty days. Although I had been in real estate for many years, none of my experience touched on multiacre historic properties. Since this seminar was close to Monticello, it was the opportune time to visit that estate and see how history was being interpreted. George and Joy Barnes agreed to accompany me on the trip.

Monticello

We visited Monticello the first day of the trip. We had contacted Dr. Dan Jordan, president of the Jefferson Foundation, ahead of time, and he and his staff made us feel very welcome. Other than Middleton Place, it was my first visit to a historic property.

First we took a tour of the Monticello house museum, which by necessity was brief since there are hundreds and maybe even thousands going through each day. By this time guides were giving extended tours that emphasized the experiences of African Americans who had been associated with Monticello. This portion was all outdoors. We viewed the sites that had housed plantation buildings used by Jefferson's slaves as they built and maintained the property. We spent most of the day there going over the extensive grounds, which included the well-known cemetery where Thomas Jefferson is buried. In the museum shop we were able to find many books relating to the lives of blacks in the historical period represented by Monticello. And, yes, the tour guides did discuss the controversy about whether or not Jefferson fathered children by his slave Sally Hemmings. It was a day packed full of education for this black man! We topped it off with a midafternoon dinner at a nearby historic tavern that serves food of Jefferson's period.

Morven Farm

The next day our "Grand Estate" seminar got under way with a tour of Morven Farm, an eight-thousand-acre estate belonging to John Kluge. As I remember, at that time Kluge was rated by *Forbes* magazine as the third wealthiest person in the United States. He was personally present to meet with our group of approximately thirty to fifty people and hosted our dinner at his carriage house.

Within the past few decades Charlottesville, Virginia, seems to have become a very desirable home location for Americans who are financially independent. The University of Virginia's location there enhances the intellectual atmosphere; the countryside is largely composed of gorgeous green rolling hills; the weather is not extreme; discriminating shoppers can locate high-end merchandise and fine antiques; award-winning vineyards and their wineries ring the small city; fine dining is available; and it's less than a two-hour drive from the nation's capital, Washington, D.C. It appears that there are many large estates that allow owners to indulge their passion for horse farms.

Participants in our seminar were headquartered at a large downtown hotel. As soon as everyone had checked in, we were transported southeast of town past the entrance to Monticello. Several miles further out, as our group approached Morven in two buses, our seminar leaders pointed out the unusual fencing that marked the beginning of the property. It seemed that most of the estates had fences with three boards running parallel to each other from top to bottom. The Morven fence lines had four, making it more secure.

There were about eight houses on the estate, as I remember, and these were significant structures, not freestanding "mother-in-law suites." In one area of the estate a large, beautiful Georgian-style home was set on a hill overlooking a private nine-hole golf course and a private chapel. A mile or so away was Kluge's historic home near Japanese gardens he had commissioned. An artistic display of statuary added another element of interest. In yet a third area of the estate John had built a twenty-five-thousand- to thirty-thousand-square-foot carriage house to store his collection of classic and historically significant horse-drawn carriages. This building included a restaurant-quality dining room, as in *fine* dining! Down the hill we noticed a helipad near a conference-center-type building designed for meetings such as the one we were attending. Still another area contained incredibly clean horse barns. Thoroughbreds were housed there, and we learned that horse breeding was one of John's businesses.

There was a reception in the carriage house for our group to view the collection before dinner. It was at this point that we met John Kluge. He's a few years older than I and very down-to-earth, an easy person with whom to talk. We immediately hit it off. He invited my group of friends and me to sit at his table for six. We had a wonderful time. He told us he had come to America as a young child with his family from Germany. During World War II, he told us, he had to defend himself against suspicions of being a Nazi sympathizer or spy although, I believe, he served in the United States armed forces. He's a self-made man as far as his fortune is concerned. From what I understand, he is involved in some businesses on an ongoing basis and makes money buying and selling them. He was still working full-time and said he never planned to retire.

Following dinner we had a seminar meeting. As I remember John and his staff were interested in furthering education about the best use of large tracts of land so as not to damage the environment.

The next day we went back to Morven from our hotel and toured some greenhouses and had a chance to hit golf balls at the nine-hole course. For people like us who live in average-sized American homes, this was like a fairy-tale adventure. Since we visited this property, Kluge has donated it to the University of Virginia.

The main point to be made here is that I was using this opportunity to begin to educate myself about a new endeavor. This is an example of my belief in lifelong learning. This particular time I was using it to do a better job in a situation unrelated to money-making, service on the board at Middleton Place, but the principle is the same either way. At seventy-seven years of age I was still learning something new—and, I might add, I was loving it!

After seven years as a trustee at Middleton Place Foundation, I retired to become trustee emeritus, and Kenny became an active trustee. Since Kenny and I have served on the board of Middleton Place Foundation, the emphasis on the interpretations of black people who have lived there throughout the property's history has definitely increased. For the first time, in November 2006, descendants of these blacks were invited to join with white Middleton descendants at the regular five-year reunion. This might have happened anyway. However, our presence may have been a reminder, if not a catalyst.

9

"Earl's getting his flowers
while he's still alive!"

For me life only gets better as it moves along. Others may make more money than me, but I can beat them living. Now in my late eighties, I feel very fortunate. I still work everyday, by choice, and my health is good. Every day of my life has been a gift from God, and I've tried to use them all in that spirit.

Early in life I figured out that for some reason in twentieth-century America the most feared and despised form of humanity was a black male. That's the body I came packaged in at birth, and I knew it would be with me all my life. I determined to live my life in a way that would change that image in the minds of people who met me, got to know me, or had any kind of business or social relationship with me. I want to dispel this negative perception of black men by making a positive impression on everyone I encounter. Of course I will not compromise my core values to do this. Fortunately my values are consistent with this endeavor.

To do this I must always have a layer in my subconscious mind that would be unnecessary if I were a white man. Has that been a burden for me, or has that been an opportunity? There has been some extra psychological weight on my shoulders, but I am enjoying this earthly journey, and indications are that I have made headway in my struggles to better the image of black men in America generally. At this time things are extremely good for me. I'm doing what I want to do; my children are doing well; three of my grandchildren, Jarae and Ashley Middleton and Alva Pearson, are college students or graduates; and my youngest grandchild, Kursten Kai Griffin, born in 2003, brings me much delight. I have much left to give.

My sister Dorothy Louise Middleton lived with me until her recent passing. This is a period in my life for enjoyment of things past, living well now, and anticipating exciting things in the time left. Hopefully I'm living my life in a way that will make it easier for the next black man who might chance to encounter someone whose life has touched mine.

As far as what I can give, for me one of the most important things is a history of my family's past. This I have been at work on, in earnest, for several years now. Throughout the thirty years that she has worked with our companies, Joy Barnes has shown an affinity for research and writing. She has been a catalyst and motivator in helping me with this project. This book derives from our endeavors in the search for my family's story.

Reunions

Reunions with those I knew years ago are always heartening, and continuing to meet new friends is something I relish. Two gentlemen come to my mind in this regard.

The first reunion came a couple of weeks after our April 1992 *Wall Street Journal* story appeared and was one of the article's positive ripple effects. It took the form of a letter with the return address of a Nashville, Tennessee, law firm. The writer was Morton Howell, a World War II captain from my Maxwell Field days. He had read the article and had wondered for all the intervening years what had happened to me. He also offered to send a photo of our Fourth Aviation Squadron at Maxwell Field. Morton and I corresponded for several years. Then in November 1999 a Middleton family reunion took me to Nashville, Tennessee, where my youngest daughter, Karen, and her husband, Kenny Griffin, live. I took the opportunity to visit Morton in his home and met his son and some friends. By this time my friend Morton was in declining health. Even so, it was obvious to me that he had valued the experience of working with our squadron of black men during World War II and that he had related this to his family through the years. I was the only one of these men any of his family had met.

Morton was unusual for his time in that he was fair to his troops regardless of race. He had, I learned recently, been born into a position of privilege. What he did with his life reminds me of the saying "To whom much is given, much is expected." He lived up to some very high expectations in all areas of his life. About six months after our Nashville reunion I received a phone call from Bill Howell, Morton's son, telling me his father had died. Bill's eulogy at his father's funeral included an account of our relationship.

Another gentleman was a new friend to me, but meeting him recently for the first time was a reunion. Let me explain this seeming paradox.

First of all in the quest to piece together my family's history, we searched for the descendants of the family who owned our relatives as slaves. There was a good possibility that a descendant might be in possession of some unpublished family records that would give us information about their slaves. South Carolina history reveals that planter families associated with and intermarried with other families of this class. Given that our surname is Middleton, my family has always assumed that members of the Arthur Middleton family owned our ancestors. Very possibly this is so. We do know, however, that the Middleton family was *not* the *last* owner of my ancestors before the Civil War ended. Because so few records were kept on slaves by name, in order to research slaves one *has* to research their owners, in whose names the records were kept. Oftentimes when a planter's daughter married she was given slaves to bring into the marriage as a part of her dower. This sometimes necessitates searching records on multiple families who might have had property interactions through marriage, inheritance, gifts, or outright sales.

At some point Joy Barnes contacted a lady in Charleston who was descended from Charles Coatsworth Pinckney, one of the South Carolina signers of the U.S. Constitution. An energetic former schoolteacher who enjoys writing, Mary Claire Pinckney Jones Seeger lives in Charleston with her husband, Bill Seeger, a Texas native and Annapolis Naval Academy graduate. Mary Claire had published her family's genealogy, and Joy and I went to visit her in our quest to learn more. She told us she knew a gentleman who was descended from a family her Pinckney ancestors had been associated with in generations past and who might be "our man." Mary Claire didn't know from which line of the family he had descended. Nonetheless she put us in touch with him, and we learned by phone that he was a direct descendant of my ancestors' owners. Joy and I scheduled a meeting with him at his home on one of the islands south of Charleston.

The fact that he was a retired air force pilot and I had trained as a pilot at Tuskegee probably contributed to the immediate rapport that developed between Edmund Bellinger and me during our initial visit of about two hours. We discussed our families' shared past, and he showed us some records and memorabilia of his family. He then exhibited a tremendous degree of trust by offering to loan us his family scrapbook, compiled by his mother over many years of his life. We accepted his generous offer, and after reading and copying it in Orangeburg, we returned it, in person, several weeks later.

It was a significant accomplishment for us to have located this new friend with connections to my family's history. About two months later, through Joy's research sleuthing, she located a previously unknown book that had been written by my grandfather Abram's brother, James B. Middleton, in 1888. In this book James describes how he got his seriously ill slave owner and his family out of their plantation home a day ahead of Sherman's army in February 1865 and safely kept them out of harm's way until he could return them home. One member of the party was the slave owner's small son. This boy was the grandfather of the new friend I had recently met.

My granduncle never named the family and referred to the slave owner as "my friend" throughout the narrative. We know who they were through the facts our research has yielded. In keeping with my uncle's precedent, I too am referring to this new acquaintance of mine as "my friend." Just as our ancestors had trusted each other 135 years ago, this same trust had somehow survived through the years. As far as I know there had been no contact between our families for at least a hundred years. Sadly for me, my friend Edmund Fishburne Bellinger Jr. unexpectedly passed away at the end of September 2001.

The Marker

The entire black Middleton family has a sense of the great worth of our history. Because Joy Barnes and I have reported on our research regularly to our extended family at reunions, we were able to agree to fund the erection of a marker in the city of Charleston celebrating our ancestors' accomplishments. Two properties at 5 and 7 President's Place have been in our family since Reconstruction. The Parsonage at number 5 was the home of my granduncle the Reverend James B. Middleton. Miss Izard's School at number 7 was the home of Harriett Middleton Izard and her family, including her daughter Anna Eliza Izard, a schoolteacher.

On May 29, 2004, we held a marker dedication ceremony, which was graciously sponsored by the Avery Research Center for African American History and Culture at the College of Charleston. Charleston mayor Joseph Riley honored us with his presence, as did Charles Duell and Dr. Eric Emerson, director of the South Carolina Historical Society. Members of our family came from far and near. Following the dedication we had a family meeting to discuss the plans for the first joint reunion of the black Middletons and the white Middletons, which was held at Middleton Place in 2006.

Errata

p. xv "Kusten Kai Griffen" should read "Kursten Kai Griffin"

p. 153 The second sentence of the final paragraph should read "In my mind, for a group of largely white local leaders in Orange burg, South Carolina, to collaborate with a dedicated cadre of black professionals to pay tribute to a black man represented success."

Celebrations

Life has been very good to me. And it goes on. In the past few years my friends and family have seen fit to honor me with some significant celebrations. As former Middleton real estate agent Geneva Roche remarked at my eightieth birthday party, "Earl's getting his flowers while he's still alive!"

In the fall of 2001 I was fortunate to receive a coveted designation from my peers and colleagues in our hometown. At the Kiwanis Club's annual banquet in September, I was named Orangeburg Citizen of the Year. During his gracious presentation remarks attorney John F. Shuler said of me: "He struggled. He didn't quit." These were the words the *Times and Democrat* used to head an article on the award. Of course Shuler and the newspaper mentioned some tangible accomplishments to my credit, such as service in World War II, legislative service, and business accomplishments. The award was a benchmark in my life. It was decided on by representatives of more than ten local civic organizations.

In February 2004 a large group of friends and family came together at Claflin University to dedicate the Earl Middleton Highway and celebrate my eighty-fifth birthday. I was particularly pleased that the proceeds from the evening went for scholarships to Claflin students. The Honorable Jerry N. Govan, a member of the S.C. House of Representatives from Orangeburg County, and Claflin president Henry N. Tisdale headed up this event. The Honorable Matthew J. Perry Jr., my old friend from civil-rights-era days and now a distinguished federal court judge, introduced me. Many of my family members came to Orangeburg for this occasion, including my niece Phyllis Middleton Jackson from South Africa.

Then in the eighty-eighth year of my life the president of the United States, George W. Bush, presented me the Congressional Gold Medal. This national honor had been awarded to all the Tuskegee Airmen at a ceremony I had missed the previous March at the Capitol Rotunda in Washington, D.C. South Carolina senator Lindsey Graham arranged for President Bush to present mine at Charleston Air Force Base on July 24, 2007.

To me these were more than personal achievements. In my mind, for a group of largely white local leaders in Orangeburg, South Carolina, to za black man represented success. Even sixty-plus years after the fact, to receive a medal personally from the commander in chief meant success. It was a success for what I represent as a black man. These were acknowledgments that as times have changed, people are changing the way they view us. To me it didn't mean that what Earl Middleton has achieved is so great and wonderful. Rather, it meant that black men could now be viewed as men, period. If knowing who I am and living the way I've lived have had a positive effect on this perception, then I have accomplished a lifelong desire. As long as God sees fit to let me live, this is what I hope to continue to do.

Earl Matthew Middleton departed this life at his home in Orangeburg, South Carolina, November 20, 2007, at the age of 88 years, 9 months, and 2 days.

Appendix I

Founding Members, Veterans of Foreign Wars,
Broadus James Jamerson Jr. Post 8166

December 11, 1952, Orangeburg, S.C.

RAYSOR ADAMS—employed at Wannamaker Pharmacy on Russell Street, drummer in a band

THEODORE R. ADAMS—employed at a local industry

EDWARD F. ANDERSON—farmer from the Orangeburg County town of Elloree

ROBERT E. BELLINGER—teacher in the public-school system and later at Claflin University

JOHN T. BLUME

LEMON M. BRADLEY

O. Z. CONLEY BRANDYBURG—merchant

ARTHUR W. BROWN

LINNIE W. CAIN—carpenter

HARLOWE E. CALDWELL—dentist who had an office next door to the Middleton Agency on Amelia Street

HENRY CARSON—painting contractor

JAMES C. CARTER

FRED CORLEY

JESSE J. COULTER—co-owner a small cab company, father of Franklin Coulter, a practicing medical doctor in Orangeburg

HENRY O. CURRY—manager our VFW post for years

WARREN C. DASH—taxi driver

CHARLES E. "CHUCK" DAVIS—teacher in the Orangeburg public schools, now living in North Carolina

ROBERT B. DYCHES—automobile worker

ALLEN ELLISON

LEON FERGUSON—electronics technician; married to Phillipine, a retired teacher

WILLIE GADSON

CHARLES D. GAFFNEY—employed at S.C. State University for most of his career

EARL R. GAFFNEY—a small-business owner

JOHNNIE E. GLOVER

PERRY GLOVER

WALTER D. GLOVER

WILLIAM GREEN

JOHN W. GREGG—teacher

THOMAS E. HAIGLER—successful painting contractor and a solid individual

MARION HARRISON—deputy sheriff in Orangeburg; married to Edna, both active in community civic affairs

MATTHEW HENDERSON—known as "Mackey," top-notch building contractor and for a time a partner with Marion Mack

WOODROW JACKSON

JEROME JENKINS

WILLIAM JENNINGS JR.

ELIJAH JOHNSON

JAMES S. JOHNSON—purchaser of my barbershop when my insurance and real estate business became full-time

JOSEPH JOHNSON—employed in horticulture with the City of Orangeburg

MALLIE JOHNSON—employed at S.C. State University

ASA JONES—electrician

SAMUEL JONES

CARL D. KENNERLY—public-school principal

MELVIN KNOTTS

ALEXANDER C. LEWIS—a close friend, masonry contractor, and public-school official

JOSEPH C. LOVE—painting contractor

JAMES MATTHEWS—owner of an electrical appliance shop on the corner of Amelia and Middleton streets

CLEOPHAS M. McCOTTRY—South Carolina native who migrated to New York

VERNON T. McDANIEL—owner of an auto business

EARL M. MIDDLETON—author of this book

ERNEST L. MONROE—businessman

EUGENE A. R. MONTGOMERY—employed at the U.S. Post Office and in the insurance business

JOSHUA O. MONTGOMERY—teacher

BRICE A. MOORER—tailoring professor at S.C. State University

CLIFFORD MURPH—business manager and farmer
ROBERT L. MURPHY
DOUGLAS O'BRYANT and DOUGLAS C. O'BRYANT—father and son
JOHN T. OLIVER
JULIUS PAUL—employed with the City of Orangeburg
NATHANIEL D. POUGH
GEORGE R. RANDOLPH—building contractor
JOHN S. ROBINSON—salesman and member of the South Carolina Real Estate Commission
WILLIAM RUSSELL SR.—valued employee at Hygrade Meat Company
ADAM SHIVERS JR.
WILMON D. SMILEY—business owner
RAYMOND SPIGNER
KIRKLAND STOKES—owner of a tailoring business
JAMES E. SULTON—businessman and community leader
GEORGE WALKER—owner of a taxi company
JULIUS I. WASHINGTON III—agribusinessman and long-time civic leader in Orangeburg
EARL W. WILLIAMS—plumbing contractor
ISAIAH WILLIAMS—businessman
JACOB C. WILLIAMS—electrician
WILFORD WILLIAMS—master carpenter
HERMAN WINNINGHAM—employed at the Savannah River nuclear facility
JAMES WRIGHT—employed at Shaw Air Force Base
SAMMIE YOUNG

Appendix 2

The "Pitts, Gerald, Messervy Delegation" to the 1956 Republican National Convention

The 1956 Republican National Convention was a turning point for blacks in determining which major party we supported. I was a member of the racially mixed South Carolina delegation to the Republican National Convention in San Francisco. The other delegation—all white as I recall—wrested control from our long-time Republican group on a technicality at the convention. It's important to know who was in our delegation and to know their qualifications. This appendix reprints a pamphlet supporting our delegation.

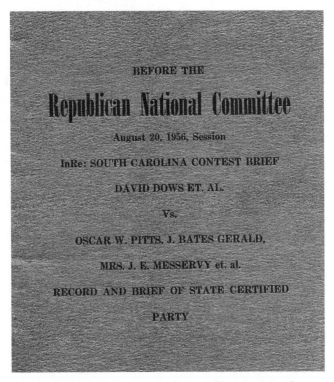

BEFORE THE

Republican National Committee

August 20, 1956, Session

InRe: SOUTH CAROLINA CONTEST BRIEF

DAVID DOWS ET. AL.

Vs.

OSCAR W. PITTS, J. BATES GERALD,

MRS. J. E. MESSERVY et. al.

RECORD AND BRIEF OF STATE CERTIFIED

PARTY

Legal brief arguing for seating the racially mixed South Carolina delegation to the 1956 Republican National Convention. Collection of the author

Delegates & Alternates of the State Certified South Carolina Republican Party Elected by State Convention, Township Auditorium, State Capital, Columbia, S.C., May 31, 1956, to represent the State of S.C. at Republican National Convention, August 20, 1956, San Mateo County, California. Proceedings broadcast over NBC Stations. Convention President Mrs. John E. Messervy," appendix to *Before the Republican National Committee, August 20, 1956, Session; In re: South Carolina Contest Brief, David Dows et al. vs. Oscar W. Pitts, J. Bates Gerald, Mrs. J. E. Messervy et al.; Record and Brief of State Certified Party* (N.p., 1956).

Mrs. John E. Messervy, Charleston, S. C.—Native of South Carolina. Prominent political and civic leader, widow of the late John E. Messervy, prominent Republican railroad director, industrialist and investment banker. Mrs. Messervy has been National Committeewoman from South Carolina continuously since 1940.

J. Bates Gerald, Charleston & Summerton, S.C.—Former State Chairman of the South Carolina Republican Party, Native South Carolinian, Past Post Commander of American Legion, Past State Vice Commander of Disabled American Veterans, member of many social and fraternal clubs, Chairman of the Board for North State Lumber Corp. Mr. Gerald's ancestral home is Camden, S.C. where since the days of the American Revolution his forebears have been distinguished leaders and pioneers in the cultural and business development of the southland.

Oscar W. Pitts, Westminster, S.C.—State Chairman South Carolina Republican Party, Native of South Carolina, Veteran of World War I, overseas service in AEF, graduate of University of South Carolina, LLB Degree, admitted to the bar in 1916. After return from World War I has been engaged in law practice in South Carolina until the present time. Has been Service Officer American Legion for 30 years. Served as member of Selective Service Board, Oconee County upon recommendation of all Veterans Organizations of the county. First cast Republican vote for Hon. Wm. Howard Taft in 1908 in Presidential Election. Elected State Chairman, State Certified South Carolina Republican Party Dec. 15, 1955, upon resignation of Hon. D. F. Merrill, re-elected State Chairman 1956 State Convention.

Dr. I. S. Leevy, Columbia, S.C.—A prominent businessman and civic leader in South Carolina, was born of humble surroundings in Antioch, Kershaw County, S.C. His formal education was pursued at Hampton

Institute, Va., where he graduated from the Industrial & Collegiate Dept. Upon graduation he came to Columbia, S.C. where he was co-organizer and founder of many worthwhile business and civic enterprises, some of which follow.

Co-organizer of the South Carolina Negro State Fair Association; Organizer of the Booker Washington School, the Waverly School and the Leevy Graded School, which at present is know as the Carver School; Co-organizer of the Richland County Tuberculosis Hospital for Negroes at Ridgewood; Co-organizer of the State Industrial School for Girls and organizer of Literary Dept. of the John G. Richards School for Negro boys located near Columbia. Mr. Leevy was instrumental in securing and was the co-organizer of the Graduate School of South Carolina State College at Orangeburg; organizer and Ex-President of the New Home Development Co.; organizer and Ex-President of the Leevy Dept. Stores of Columbia; organizer and President of the Standard Furniture Co.; organizer and Ex-President of the Victory Savings Bank; Ex-Vice President of the National Negro Bankers Association of America; organizer and manager of Leevy's Esso Service Station, the first such owned and operated by a Negro in this area. Leevy organized the Negro Mortuary Dept. of the South Carolina State Hospital, and his persistence in petitioning for a Negro chaplain at the aforesaid institution has resulted in the appointment of same.

At present Mr. Leevy is President of the Lincoln Emancipation Clubs, Inc., which he founded and organized. He is organizer and President of the Hunter Investment, Inc. of Columbia, S.C. He is President and Manager of Leevy's Funeral Home; is Richland County Chairman of the South Carolina Republican Party and State director of Publicity of the same. As a Republican he has been 3 times a candidate for the Columbia City Council, 2 times a candidate for the South Carolina Legislature and 3 times a candidate for the United States Congress. Having been recently named as delegate-at-large to the Republican National Convention to be held in California in August where candidates for President and Vice-President for the United States will be nominated, his prominence in the National Political scene is being felt.

Because of his great success and civic leadership, the Doctor of Humanities Degree was bestowed upon him by Morris College in Sumter, SC.; the MS Degree was awarded him by South Carolina State College of Orangeburg; the Dr. of Laws Degree was bestowed upon him by Allen University, Columbia, S.C. in 1956.

Dr. George G. Daniels—Prominent leader, President of Baptist State Convention, Corresponding Secretary of the National Baptist Convention, President of the Board of Trustees, Morris College.

Mr. Earl Middleton, Orangeburg, S.C.—Prominent businessman, civic and church leader.

Mrs. Ruth K. Pitts, Westminster, S.C.—Native Southerner, Income Tax Consultant, first presidential vote ever cast was in 1936 for Hon. Alfred M. Landon; been member Oconee County Republican Organization since 1934; member of State Central Committee South Carolina Republican Party since 1950; former state Vice-Chairman.

Mrs. Elizabeth P. Cherry, Charleston, S.C.—State Vice-Chairman, widow of Hon. G. J. Cherry, former national Committeeman of South Carolina Republican Party; President of North State Lumber Corp. and several others; County Chairman of Charleston County Unit, the South Carolina Republican Party and member of the State Executive Committee.

Mrs. Frances Jones, Charleston, S.C.—Long time member of the South Carolina Republican Party; Secretary Charleston county Organization. Delegate to the 1956 Republican National Convention.

Rev. St. Justin Simpkins, Charleston S.C.—Rector St. James Episcopal Church, Charleston, S.C.; long-time Republican. Delegate to the 1956 Republican National Convention.

Mr. George H. Hampton, Columbia, South Carolina—Publisher and owner *The Palmetto Leader Weekly Newspaper,* Director Victory Savings Bank, prominent businessman and Republican of Columbia, S.C.

Mr. Charles C. Manson, Charleston S.C.—Prominent businessman, mortician and loyal Republican.

Mrs. H. Z. Wolfe, Williston, S.C.—Prominent church and social leader, Barnwell County; former member of Young Republican County Chairman, Barnwell County Unit of Republican Party for many years. Elected Secretary of State Convention and delegate to the National Convention.

Rev. I. DeQuincey Newman, Sumter, S.C.—District Superintendent Methodist Church and responsible businessman Sumter, S.C. elected delegate to National Convention.

Rev. J. Herbert Nelson—Preacher, Professor and reputable businessman, Latta, S.C.

Mr. C. M. Smith, Walhalla, S.C.—Native South Carolinian, life long Republican and has been County Chairman in Oconee County since 1928. Member of State Executive Committee and delegate to National Convention. Candidate for Congress 1954.

Mr. C. Lee Davis, Anderson, S.C.—President of Baptist Layman's Association of South Carolina, Prominent Businessman, mortician and civic leader, elected delegate to National Convention.

Mr. Pat Garnett, Columbia, S.C.—Born in San Saba, Texas, July 5, 1914; Father native of Edgefield, S.C. was minister in Texas and married in San Antonio. Mr. Garnett moved to Greenville, S.C. at 11 years of age; attended Wofford College, Furman University and Juilliard School of Music. Received degree in Music from Teachers College, Columbia, University of New York. Has taught for the past 20 years in Spartanburg, Gaffney, Greenville, Parker and most recently Dreher High School, Columbia, City School System. Will be band and music instructor at the University of South Carolina in Columbia at beginning of the next school term.

Rev. L. C. Jenkins—Pastor of Union Baptist Church of Columbia, Secretary of State Baptist Convention. Prominent leader of Columbia, S.C.; long time Republican, elected delegate to National Convention.

Mrs. Lena R. Bellotte, Greenville S.C.—Life-time Republican native born Southerner, businesswoman of Greenville; County Chairman Greenville County Republican Party; candidate for Congress nominated by State Certified Republican Party in 1954. Elected Secretary South Carolina Republican Party Dec. 15, 1955 to fill un-expired [term] of W.B. Wilson who resigned; re-elected State Secretary at State Convention by vote of all the State Execution Committee in compliance with South Carolina Election Law.

Dr. W. M. Porter—Life-long Republican; pharmacist, civic and church leader, Spartanburg, S.C.

Mrs. Evelyn N. Tingle—Prominent business and social leader, Greenville, S.C. Served as Secretary Greenville County Unit of Party for several terms.

Mr. John S. Woodward—Mortician, businessman, fraternal and church worker and business leader of Spartanburg S.C. Member State Executive Committee of Spartanburg.

Rev. F. G. C. Dubois—Methodist Minister, prominent citizen and businessman, Route1, Camden, S.C. Former member of Young Republican Club. Grandson of last Negro postmaster is South Carolina.

Mr. W. B. Clemons—Mortician, prominent fraternal and civic leader; active in church work, Rock Hill, S.C. Member of State Executive Committee.

Mr. James Alexander—Prominent Negro businessman and leader Camden, S.C. Member State Executive Committee, elected alternative delegate.

Mrs. Lucy B. Clemons—Assists husband in his work as mortician, Rock Hill, S.C. Social and church leader and alternative delegate.

Mr. Chives Prosser—Businessman, long-time Republican; native of S.C., elected State Treasurer Dec. 15, 1955 to fill un-expired term of W. Tate Baggett who resigned. Re-elected State Treasurer State Convention May 31, 1956 to serve for next 2 years. Delegate from 5th District to National Convention. County Chairman, Florence County.

Dr. W. S. Thompson—Prominent Negro Dentist and outstanding businessman, Georgetown, S.C. has been County Chairman for many years. Elected delegate from 6th District.

Mr. R. B. Anderson—Former clerk in Post Office and city mail carrier. Classmate of Dr. I. S. Leevy of Hampton Institute in Va. Mr. Anderson's father was a member of the S.C. Legislature and postmaster both life-long Republicans and Native South Carolinians.

Appendix 3

Wall Street Journal, *April 29, 1992*

Reprinted from THE WALL STREET JOURNAL.

WEDNESDAY, APRIL 29, 1992

Fair Trade

A Black Entrepreneur Vaults Racial Barriers In a Southern Town

Earl Middleton, Descendant Of Slaves, Sells Houses To White and Black Alike

The Difficult Early Years

By DOROTHY J. GAITER
Staff Reporter of THE WALL STREET JOURNAL

ORANGEBURG, S.C. — The white woman in his office was asking him for a job, and Earl Middleton was scared.

"I was afraid to hire her, afraid to ride in a car with her for fear that whites would think I wanted to rape her," says Mr. Middleton, a real-estate broker.

But Mr. Middleton did hire Joy Barnes 20 years ago — and several other whites since then. Today, the descendant of slaves runs the largest real-estate agency in this community of 50,000 people, about 40% of whom are white.

In an area where blacks and whites still have little social contact, and where neighborhoods are still largely segregated, Mr. Middleton's

Earl Middleton

agency sells homes all over — including the posh area that surrounds the local country club, which has no black members. Half of Mr. Middleton's customers and employees are white, half are black. One agent is the daughter of a Klansman. Another, the mother of a black county councilman.

Success has placed the 73-year-old Mr. Middleton, a tall, dignified, pipe-smoking man, in the forefront of black entrepreneurs now beginning to achieve a long-elusive goal — building businesses that cut across racial lines. While blacks now own more than 424,000 businesses in the U.S., most still cater almost entirely to black customers. But some are finding ways to reach a broader — and often more affluent — market.

How Mr. Middleton achieved this goal is partly a story of shifting race relations in the South. But it's also the tale of a determined and hard-working entrepreneur making his own luck, seizing opportunities and running hard with them. Mr. Middleton capitalized on the growth of a black middle class here, as well as an influx of whites from the North and West, who sometimes brought more tolerant attitudes. And he got help from the federal government and a few white business leaders.

Secret of Success

"I just like people," Mr. Middleton says of his success. "Black or white, it doesn't matter to me. It never did. And I work hard."

But like others, Mr. Middleton endured rebuffs and humiliations.

"Some of the things you're asking me to remember, I've been trying hard to forget," he says. "You almost had to be subservient. You had to sell your dignity almost. If you think about it, it'll almost make you cry." After a pause, he adds: "If we were little people and didn't know who we were, we could have become discouraged."

Initially, Mr. Middleton and Eugene Montgomery, a partner he later bought out, had plenty of reason to feel discouraged. They began selling homes and insurance as a sideline from the back of Mr. Middleton's barbershop. At first, they couldn't find a single white or black insurance company that would list them as a representative.

Even so, they took applications for insurance. Then they went to a "friendly" white agent, who processed the forms through his company and took 10% to 15% of the commission. The policies would come back with the white agent's stamp, "and we would put our stamp over that so no one would know," Mr. Middleton says. "It was embarrassing."

Survive, Then Thrive

Over the years, Middleton & Associates found other ways to survive and then prosper. Today, it has about 20% of the local real-estate market and is often the sales leader of the town's 14 agencies, says Jeannine Kees, a competing agent who keeps statistics on local real-estate sales. Seven years ago, it became the first black-owned affiliate of Sears, Roebuck & Co.'s Coldwell Banker. Now Mr. Middleton's son Kenneth, 36, is expanding the firm.

Mr. Middleton says the roots of his success go back to his great-great-grandfather, a slave purchased by the Middleton family of Charleston and assigned to the master's sons as a valet. The sons shared their studies with their valet and insisted he accompany them to Oxford University. According to a biography of the family, "Lemon Swamp and Other Places," written by the slave's descendants, the valet became proficient in Hebrew and Greek.

Once home, he taught members of his family, who in turn taught others.

Today, Earl Middleton says an emphasis on training and education has been one factor in his agency's success. His son has a degree in business and teaches a real-estate course, and many of the other agents have college degrees and advanced real-estate certifications.

By the time Earl Matthew Middleton was born, the youngest of six children, the family was already well-known and respected by blacks and whites in Orangeburg. Earl's father was a carpenter, and his mother belonged to the first graduating class of South Carolina State University, one of two predominantly black colleges here.

Early in life, Earl showed a knack for getting along with people. "He was never taught to hate whites," says Alexander Lewis, a childhood friend.

As a boy, he cut the lawns and scrubbed the floors of rich whites, whose sons eventually grew up to be business and civic leaders. He played marbles with Walker Limehouse, who later founded a local savings and loan association that made loans to Mr. Middleton's black clients when other financial institutions wouldn't.

"I've known Earl since early childhood, and that was a big help," says Mr. Limehouse. But, he adds, the savings and loan was a community-oriented institution: "We were chartered that way, and it was just good business."

Later, Mr. Middleton studied sociology, excelled in sports and became class president each of his four years at Claflin College, a small, predominantly black Methodist school here.

No Teaching or Preaching

In 1942, Mr. Middleton entered the armed forces, first training at Tuskegee, Ala., to become a pilot and then, when he didn't make the final cut, joining the Army. There, as part of a segregated unit, he cut black servicemen's hair. Home again in 1946, and wanting to do something besides "teaching or preaching," he got a job at a barbershop. The following year, he bought his own barbershop and married Bernice Bryant, his brainy longtime sweetheart. In addition to Kenneth, they have two daughters, Anita, a reading specialist, and Karen, a university athletic trainer.

Mr. Middleton's real-estate and insurance sideline did little business in the early years. Unaccustomed to black agents, well-off blacks took their business to white-owned firms, he says. But a turning point came one day when a black customer nodded off during a haircut. Mr. Middleton says poor whites used to buy insurance from him because they feared white agents would look down on them. When the black customer awoke, he was shocked to find three white men buying insurance. "He said, 'Earl, I didn't know you sold insurance to white people. You must be good,' " Mr. Middleton recalls.

Still, in the early 1960s, buying and selling homes continued to be difficult. "Sometimes we were afraid to send blacks up to the banks," Mr. Middleton says. Occasionally, bank officers tried to discourage them. "Oh, you don't want to buy out there. There's swamp out there," he recalls one saying.

Situations like that wore on Mr. Middleton's dignity. "You almost had to agree with them, go along with what they would say, laugh at their jokes," he says with pain in his voice. "It was unbelievable. You had no alternative." The bank officer might reject the buyer because he was black. Antagonizing him assured rejection.

"They [whites] knew what owning a home meant," he says. "That's pride. That's spirit. If a man gets a house, that means he's somebody. If a man has spirit that means he'll do some things that others won't do."

Desegregation has come slowly and grudgingly to Orangeburg. Around 1960, Mr. Middleton signed a petition to send his daughter Anita to an all-white high school. Mr. Lewis, his best friend, did the same for his son, and ended up losing his bricklaying company, which employed 11 black men. The only black business owners who were spared, Mr. Lewis says, had predominantly black clienteles, such as funeral home directors and barbers, including Mr. Middleton.

In this period, Mr. Middleton, a life member of the National Association for the Advancement of Colored People, joined a sit-in that permanently closed a local variety store. Mrs. Middleton, who headed South Carolina State's library science department, was arrested and bused 45 miles to jail in Columbia for joining a student protest. "We filled the jail" in Orangeburg, she says proudly.

Race relations hit bottom on Feb. 8, 1968. State patrolmen fatally shot three unarmed students and wounded 27 on South Carolina State's campus. The students were protesting the whites-only policy of a nearby bowling alley. The nine patrolmen tried in the deaths were found not guilty.

But new federal civil rights laws started to help Mr. Middleton's business. It became easier for blacks to get loans. And a person selling a home could no longer legally refuse a buyer solely because of race. Government agencies sent testers to ferret out discrimination in housing.

Help Arrives

Mr. Middleton soon got two big breaks from the federal government: contracts to manage and sell foreclosed properties for both the Federal Housing Administration and the Veterans Administration. The contracts accounted for most of his real-estate business for several years. And as whites became interested in buying these properties, Mr. Middleton was the person to see.

"They saw that I could speak properly, that I dressed well, I wasn't a fool, didn't smell and didn't get drunk on Saturdays—all those myths — and they said, 'I don't know who he is but he knows his stuff,' " Mr. Middleton says.

Later, two white lumber-company owners, J.R. and Charles Council, decided to help Mr. Middleton. Charles also owned a development company, and his brother, J.R., was president of Mr. Limehouse's savings and loan. When Charles's company built a middle-class subdivision in a black area, he insisted that Mr. Middleton sell some of the homes — an important break, Mr. Middleton says.

In some ways, the most dramatic change in Mr. Middleton's businesses began in 1972, when the white real-estate agent, Joy Barnes, asked for a job.

"Sure, people thought I was crazy," recalls Ms. Barnes. "But I saw what kind of potential was there because of the man who was involved." She noticed the demographics, too, especially the predominantly black colleges "sitting there full of Ph.D.s."

White and Black Clubs

Ms. Barnes did have one worry: She belonged to an all-white country club. "I asked [Mr. Middleton] if he minded and he said, no, he belonged to an all-black club," she recalls.

At first, Ms. Barnes says, whites often told her they wouldn't list with a black company. Sometimes when she called a white-owned agency to ask if she could show one of its listings, the agent would ask her client's race. She says she always answered the same way: " 'Why do you ask?' And they would drop it. They had to because it was against the law."

The agency also profited from a growing willingness here to put practicality over racial politics. "Business is business and politics is politics," says Robert Agee, director of research and development for an Ethyl Corp. chemical plant here, who has bought two homes through the Middleton agency. "Regardless of what you feel about race relations, you have a family you're responsible for, so value in real estate just supersedes feelings about race."

The Middleton Agency sells energetically and is willing occasionally to cut its commission or absorb extra costs to get a sale, its agents say. For instance, the agency sold a house to Jeff and Bessie Dowling for $68,900. But the four-bedroom, two-bath home needed repairs. Because the seller refused either to reduce his asking price or to make the repairs, the Middleton agency paid to have the job done.

Before the Dowlings could get their utilities turned on, they either had to pay a deposit or get a resident to sign for them. Kenneth Middleton signed. "He didn't have to do that but he trusted us and we appreciated that," says Ms. Dowling.

The Dowlings are part of another helpful trend: the growing number of blacks re-

turning to Orangeburg. While Mr. Dowling is stationed overseas in the Navy, Mrs. Dowling wanted to return to her alma mater, South Carolina State, to pursue a graduate degree.

In 1977, after Kenneth graduated from Furman College, the senior Mr. Middleton began turning over the real-estate business to his son, while focusing personally on insurance and real-estate management.

Earl and Bernice Middleton still live in the modest home they bought more than 30 years ago for about $13,000 and later expanded. Age has forced him to give up quail and partridge hunting, but he still fishes and takes out his small boat from his second home on the waterfront in Santee, 20 miles from Orangeburg.

The younger Mr. Middleton, whose wife is an engineer, takes a New South approach. "If the spread of services is sufficient, the color line disappears," he says. "We simply had to believe that if we gave superior service for a significant time, it's like water on a rock, like the Berlin Wall, it just had to come down."

Even today, Mr. Middleton is caught sometimes in the middle of racial tensions. Some of the agency's white salespeople say they sometimes are asked why they work for a black firm. And, Mr. Middleton says, some white agencies have told white sellers that the Middletons engage in "blockbusting"—breaking up white neighborhoods—which they deny.

"I wish we could take all the credit for integrated neighborhoods, but we can't," says Kenneth Middleton.

At the same time, some blacks question Mr. Middleton's comfortable relations with whites. "Earl doesn't ruffle feathers," says Bernard Haire, a black member of the city council who is known as a radical. "It's hard for me to make compromises with white folks. He's able to do that. I'm hard-nosed. I've lived in Orangeburg all my life, and there's too much that we're not a part of."

Replies Mr. Middleton: "Compromise is a pretty strong word. I didn't compromise. I had tact and you had to have it."

But racial tensions haven't kept Mr. Middleton from expanding his business. The 14-member sales force is diverse enough to reach nearly any group. The top salesperson last year was Geneva Roache, a black woman whose husband is a retired South Carolina State dean. Maggie Rickenbacker is a black grandmother with a master's degree. Her husband is a minister and her son is a member of the county council.

Virgie Fields and Vivian Rutland are white women who live on farms and can talk knowledgeably about farm land.

Then there's Anne Jameson. She says her late father was a Klansman — "but he never did anything that actually hurt people." Whites who knew him tell her, "If your daddy could see you now, he would spin in his grave,' " she says. "And he would. But he's not here now."

Sources

This book is my memoir, but Joy Barnes and I believed from the beginning that, because my life has been touched by so much history and because I wanted to tell about some of my ancestors, my story would be enhanced if we consulted other people and written sources. For these reasons we are including this list of sources, which are cited according to the order in which they relate to the text.

For a comprehensive history of Orangeburg, I'd suggest Dean Livingston's *Yesteryears . . . : A Newsman's Look Back at the Events and People Who Have Influenced the Histories of Orangeburg and Calhoun Counties* (Orangeburg, S.C.: Trippett Press, 2006). For information included in several chapters, we consulted *The South Carolina Encyclopedia,* edited by Walter Edgar (Columbia: University of South Carolina Press, 2006).

Chapter 1—Ancestors

Bellinger, Joseph. Estate inventory. Charleston District (S.C.) Inventory Book G (1824–34), 377–78, 380–81.

Charles R. Carroll Papers. South Caroliniana Library, University of South Carolina, Columbia.

Patterson, Isabel. *Builders of Freedom and Their Descendants.* Augusta, Ga.: Walton Printing Company, 1953, 104.

Bellinger, Edmund C. Will. Charleston County (S.C.) Will Book K (1845–51), 227.

Gutman, Herbert G. *The Black Family in Slavery and Freedom.* New York: Vintage, 1976, 153.

Carroll, F. F., to Abram Middleton. Deed. May 6, 1868. Bamberg (S.C.) County Courthouse.

Dryden, Felicia Furman. *Historical Sketch and Workbook—Families Associated with Woodlands Plantation.* N.p.: Privately published, 1999, 4.

Jenkins, Warren. *Steps Along the Way.* Columbia, S.C.: Socamead Press, 1967, 8, 66–67.

Curry, John W. *Passionate Journey: History of the 1866 South Carolina Annual Conference.* St. Matthews, S.C.: Bill Wise Printers, 1980, 10, 16.

Middleton, Benjamin W. In Registers of Signatures of Depositors. Card No. 6195. Freedman's Savings and Trust Co., Charleston Branch, NA, RG 101, Microcopy 816, Roll 22, South Carolina Archives and History Center, Columbia.

Records of Appointments of Postmasters, 1832–1971. NARA, M 841, roll 114, Barnwell County, S.C., 29:976–77.

Bryant, Dr. Lawrence C., ed. *Negro Lawmakers in the South Carolina Legislature, 1868–1902.* Orangeburg: School of Graduate Studies, S.C. State College, 1968, 9–10.

Foner, Eric. *Freedom's Lawmakers: A Directory of Black Officeholders during Reconstruction.* New York: Oxford University Press, 1993, 149.

Family record. Abram Middleton family Bible (1851), owned in 2006 by Pauline Mansfield.

Middleton, Abraham, household. 1900 U.S. Census, Orangeburg County, S.C. Orange Township, enumeration district [ED] 67, supervisor's district [SD] 243, sheet 22 A & B, line 39, dwelling 308, family 434, National Archives micropublication T 623, roll CN321.

Govan, Paul, household. 1900 U.S. Census, Orangeburg County, S.C. Orange Township, enumeration district [ED] 67, supervisor's district [SD] 243, sheet 22 B, line 52, dwelling 309, family 435, National Archives micropublication T 623, roll CN321.

Catalogue of the Colored Normal, Industrial and Mechanical College of South Carolina Located at Orangeburg, 1904–1905. Orangeburg, S.C.: Printed by W. F. Cannon, 1905, 90.

Franklin, John H., and Alfred A. Moss Jr. *From Slavery to Freedom—A History of African Americans,* 7th ed. New York: Knopf, 1994, 354.

Gore, Blinzy L. *On a Hilltop High—The Origin and History of Claflin College to 1984.* Spartanburg, S.C.: Reprint Company, 1994.

Hendren, Lee. "Orangeburg Eyes Population Growth through Annexation," *Orangeburg Times and Democrat,* August 13, 2006, 1.

Obituary for Capt. Samuel Middleton, *Orangeburg Times and Democrat,* February 21, 1952.

"Orangeburg Man's Roots Run Deep at Middleton Place," *Orangeburg Times and Democrat,* July 28, 2002, 7.

Barnes, Joy W. Interview with Phillip G. Middleton, August 1, 2006.

Sabb, Cynthia B. Telephone interview with Carmen E. Brown, granddaughter of Dr. Seibels Remington Green, July 25, 2006.

———. Telephone interview with Rene Hamilton, secretary of Trinity United Methodist Church in Orangeburg, S.C., July 31, 2006.

Barnes, Joy W. Telephone interview with Josephine Freeland Shuler (Mrs. J. F. Shuler), July 26, 2006.

Grit—Stories of American Life & Traditions. http://www.grit.com/history/ (accessed August 1, 2006).

Marion Middleton et al. v. Samuel Middleton. Judgment roll 169, no. 18, State of South Carolina, County of Orangeburg, September 12, 1918, G. L. Salley, Clerk of Court.

Chapter 2—Impressions

Christian, Charles M. *Black Saga: The African American Experience—A Chronology.* Washington, D.C.: Civitas/Counterpoint, 1999, 86.

Fitchett, Horace. "The Claflin College Graduate and the Community," *Negro History Bulletin* 8 (October 1944): 11.

Burroughs, Tony. *Black Roots—A Beginner's Guide to Tracing the African American Family Tree.* New York: Simon & Schuster, 2001, 287.

Glover, Vivian. *Men of Vision—Claflin College and Her Presidents.* Orangeburg, S.C.: Bill Wise Printers, 1995.

Egerton, John. *Speak Now against the Day: The Generation Before the Civil Rights Movement in the South.* New York: Knopf, 1994, 110–20.

Chapter 3—Working for My White Uncle

Ramsey, Mike. "Restoration of Owens Field Hangar Likely," *State,* December 26, 2001, B1.

Holman, Lynn M., and Thomas Reilly. *The Tuskegee Airmen.* Charleston, S.C.: Arcadia Publishing, 1998, 7.

Dryden, Charles W. *A-Train: Memoirs of a Tuskegee Airman.* Tuscaloosa: University of Alabama Press, 1997, 110.

Harris, Jacqueline. *The Tuskegee Airmen: Black Heroes of World War II.* Parsippany, N.J.: Dillon Press, 1996, 24–25.

Motley, Mary P. *The Invisible Soldier: The Experience of the Black Soldier, World War II.* Detroit: Wayne State University Press, 1975, 198–99.

Holway, John B. *Red Tails Black Wings: The Men of America's Black Air Force.* Las Cruces, N.M.: Yucca Tree Press, 1997, 126.

Gailey, Harry A. *The War in the Pacific from Pearl Harbor to Tokyo Bay.* Novato, Calif.: Presidio Press, 1995, 433–35, 486–97.

Cook, Janet Rynolds. "General MacArthur's Surrender Order to the Japanese." Based on information provided by Charlie Barrow, son of M.Sgt. Lawrence A. Burrow. http://www.cneti.com/-chs/message.htm (accessed November 6, 2001).

Osur, Alan M. *Blacks in the Army Air Forces during World War II: The Problem of Race Relations.* Washington, D.C.: Office of Air Force History, 1977.

Chapter 4—Orangeburg

Thompson, Marilyn W. "Stories, Letters Link Thurmond, Woman," *Washington Post,* August 5, 1992, A1, A13.

"Thurmond's Bi-racial Daughter Steps Forward to Claim Heritage," *Orangeburg Times and Democrat,* December 18, 2003, 1.

Washington-Williams, Essie Mae, and William Stadiem. *Dear Senator: A Memoir by the Daughter of Strom Thurmond.* New York: Regan Books, 2005.

Nance Birthday Celebration Program, *Biography of M. Maceo Nance, Jr.,* March 28, 1986.

Robert, Joseph C. *Ethyl: A History of the Corporation and the People Who Made It.* Charlottesville: University Press of Virginia, 1983, 189.

"Zeus, About Us, 40 Years of Innovation," http://www.zeusinc.com/about_us.asp (accessed January 5, 2007).

Claflin University. "The Claflin History," http://www.claflin.edu/AboutUs/Claflin History.html (accessed January 7, 2007).

Chapter 5—Being My Own Boss

Barnes, Joy W. Interview with Linneaus C. Dorman, July 8, 2002.

South Carolina Business Hall of Fame. *Legacy of Leadership—I. S. Leevy (1876–1968)*, video segment and text, http://www.myetv.org/television/productions/legacy/laureates/issac%2 . . . (accessed August 12, 2006).

Barnes, Joy W. Telephone interviews with I. S. Leevy Johnson, June 28, 2002 and June 6, 2007.

———. Telephone interview with Greg Shorey, July 2, 2002.

Chapter 6—Overcoming the System

South Carolina Archives and History Center. *African American National Register Sites & Historical Markers in South Carolina, March 2002.* Columbia, S.C.: South Carolina Archives and History Center, 2002, 20.

Barnes, Joy W. Telephone interview with Cecil J. Williams, July 22, 2006.

———. Interview with Anita Middleton Pearson, August 11, 2006.

Downtown Orangeburg Revitalization Association. *Orangeburg . . . : A Small Town with a Big History.* Orangeburg, S.C., ca. 2006.

Foner, Jack D. *Blacks and the Military in American History: A New Perspective.* New York: Praeger, 1974, 203.

Chapter 7—Decade of Progress

"The Times and Democrat—History and Origins," http://en.wikipedia.org/wiki/The_Times_and_Democrat (accessed August 11, 2006).

Jordan, Vernon E., Jr. "South Faces New Era—Dixie Can Lead Nation in Quest for Racial Equality," *State,* April 6, 1976.

Chapter 8—Business in the Next Generation

Barnes, Joy W. Telephone interview with Jaime Harrison, January 13, 2007.

Fields, Mamie Garvin, and Karen Fields. *Lemon Swamp and Other Places: A Carolina Memoir.* New York: Free Press, 1983.

Chapter 9—"Earl's getting his flowers while he's still alive!"

Middleton, J. B. *Reminiscences and Biographical Sketches of the South Carolina Conference of the Methodist Episcopal Church.* Atlanta: Clark University Press, 1888, 8–16.

Hendren, Lee. "'He Struggled. He Didn't Quit': Earl Middleton named 'Citizen of the Year,'" *Orangeburg Times and Democrat,* September 14, 2001, A3.

———. "OUTSTANDING—Gala Celebrates Earl Middleton's Life, Achievements," *Orangeburg Times and Democrat,* February 23, 2004, A1.

Index

race relations: and Middleton family, 14, 15–17, 26–28, 78, 80–83, 92; in S.C. House, 114–15; EM's views on, 35–37, 78, 80–82, 153. *See also* segregation
racism, 51–53, 65–66, 82–83
Randolph, A. Philip, 46
Randolph, Joseph B., 22–23
real estate business, 19
Reconstruction Era, 5, 110
Regional Medical Center, Orangeburg, S.C., 7
Reilly, Thomas, 46
Republican Party, 29–30, 127; National Convention of 1956, 85–86, 159–64
Revolutionary War, 6
Richards, Johnny, 49
Richardson (contractor), 19
Ricklefs, Roger, 140
Riley, Joseph, 152
Riley, Richard W., 120
Roberts, Ralph, 133
Robinson, Curtis C., 45–46
Robinson, John, 96
Robinson, Sugar Ray, 49–50
Roche, Geneva, 153
Roosevelt, Eleanor, 46, 81
Roosevelt, Franklin D., 46, 55
Rose, Sherman, 42, 45
Rothchild (air corps lieutenant), 49
Rush, Betty, 78–79
Russell (air corps sergeant), 49

St. Stephen United Methodist Church, 80
Sanford, Mark, 101, 113
San Francisco, Calif., 85–86, 159–64
Santee Cooper Public Service Authority, 72
SCANA group, 139
school desegregation, 81
Scott, Vivian, 63
Scottsboro Boys, 51
Seeger, Bill, 151

Seeger, Mary Claire Pinckney Jones, 151
segregation: beginnings in S.C., 90; black education and, 6; of Boy Scout troops, 79; on buses, 51–52; in doctor's offices, 116; in education, 95; and employment discrimination, 65–66; impact on black social structures, 70; impact on EM's business tactics, 82–83; indignities of, 95; Middleton family attitude toward, 26–28; in military, 50, 54, 56; at Orangeburg fairgrounds, 15; on passenger trains, 35–37; in professional organizations, 105; in sports, 67
Selective Service Board, 102
Sellers, Bakari, 101
Sellers, Cleveland, 101
September 11, 2001, attacks, 25–26
Shealy, Rod, 126
Shecut, James C., 93–94
Sheheen, Robert, 125
Shelor, Robert, 49
Shepherd, Chester D., 49, 53, 63
Sherman, William T., 6, 97, 152
Shuler, Josephine Freeland, 16
Sifly family, 16
Silver Beaver Award (Boy Scouts), 123
Silver Grill, Orangeburg, S.C., 24–25
Simms, William Gilmore, 3
Simkins, Modjeska, 29
Simpkins, St. Justin, 162
Sims, James L., 110–11
slavery, 19, 21–22, 28, 89, 144–45
sloyd (manual art), 28
Smith, C. M., 163
Smith, Ed "Cotton," 30
Smith, Hampton D., 41
Smith, Henry E., 100
South Carolina: automobile license renewal, 116–17; black voter registration, 103; circuit judge appointments, 122–23; death penalty reinstatement, 113–14;